APARTMENT KITCHEN GARDENING

A Guide to Growing Food Without a Garden of Your Own

JAMES JACQUES

First published 2022
Copyright © 2022

Pelargonium Press
www.pelargoniumpress.com

All rights reserved. No part of this publication may be reproduced or transmitted in any form or by any means, electronic or mechanical, including photocopying, recording, or any information storage or retrieval system, without prior permission in writing from the publishers.

ISBN: 978-1-7396849-0-7

Illustrations by Diane Holmes
(artbydiane.co.uk)

CONTENTS

Introduction   v

PART I
GROWING IN AN APARTMENT

1. Fundamentals   3
   Growing Medium   4
   Project: Regrow Herbs and Veg   7
   Water   10
   Nutrition   12
   Light   14
   Temperature   17
2. Getting Started   23
   Apartment Gardening Gear   24
   Starting from Seed   29
   Growing in Containers   32
   Project: Upcycled Bottle Pots   33

PART II
CHOOSING YOUR PLANTS

3. Vegetables   37
   Cool Season Veg   38
   Warm Season Veg   51
   Mushrooms   59
4. Herbs   64
5. Fruit   72
   Project: Pineapple   79
6. Other Edibles   81

PART III
GROWING PLACES

7. Apartment Growing Zones   91
   Windowsills   92
   Window Boxes   94
   Bathroom   96

Balcony	97
Walls and Ceilings	99
8. Above and Beyond	101
Rooftop Gardening	102
Community and Allotment Gardens	104
Garden Sharing	107

PART IV
TAKING THINGS FURTHER

9. Soil Science	111
Mixing Media	112
Homemade Compost	115
Project: Wormery	119
10. Advanced Equipment	121
Grow Lights	122
Heating	125
Hydroponic Kits	128
Conclusion	133

INTRODUCTION

"He who sees things grow from the beginning will have the best view of them"
  – Aristotle

Imagine the moment of delight as you sit down to a delicious meal made from produce you grew yourself. Perhaps it is a crisp, leafy salad with grated carrot and a herb dressing, topped with juicy tomatoes, straight from the vine. Perhaps it's a chilli made with your own jalapeños. Perhaps it's a creamy mushroom stroganoff with your own gourmet oyster mushrooms, garnished with fresh chives. The possibilities are vast. You tuck in, proud of what you have achieved and amazed by the flavour of the healthy produce you have grown. And most remarkable of all? You grew it in your apartment.

It's hard to overstate the benefits of growing your own food, and in arriving at this book, you likely already have your own mix of reasons for wanting to start or expand your home production. You may be looking to enjoy something that is fresh, nutritious and tasty. You might be wanting to exert more control over what you put into your body. You might be looking for a fun project to do with the kids. Or you might simply appreciate the joy of planting a seed and watching something grow, making your home a greener, more interesting place to live and supporting your wellbeing. You can reap all of these rewards and more through your own kitchen gardening projects.

More and more people are turning to growing their own food as a way to improve their lifestyle, and many are lucky to have a patch of ground, either in their own garden or in an allotment, in which to produce their own bounty. But what if you don't? What if you are one of the millions of people who lives in an apartment, without the luxury of a patch of earth in which to grow stuff? Fear not! You don't have to miss out, and this book is for you. In fact, there are loads of ways you can still grow fabulous fruit, vegetables and herbs indoors, outside your windows, and, if you're fortunate enough to have one, on a balcony. Even if you do live in a house with a garden and are just looking to bring some of the gardening fun inside and expand your growing season, this book is for you too. Let's take the meaning of home grown to a whole new level. You can even grow ingredients for your kitchen in your kitchen – now that's what I call kitchen gardening!

If you've never grown a thing in your life or if you've never grown indoors before, don't worry. At the start of the book, I'm going to take you through the basics of growing and the key things you need to know about inside growing conditions. We're then going to get adventurous and look at a whole host of fun and creative ways to get growing in and around your apartment. I have been growing food both indoors and outdoors for many years and I look forward to sharing my tips and tricks with you.

PART I
GROWING IN AN APARTMENT

Let's kick off by looking at the basics of growing food. In this section, we are going to cover the core knowledge and essential equipment you need to be an apartment kitchen gardener. You'll soon see that the principles behind growing great food are relatively straightforward and you don't need a lot of kit to get started.

CHAPTER 1
FUNDAMENTALS

Irrespective of what and where you are growing, there are a few fundamentals if you want to end up with a strong, successful crop. These are:

- A growing medium, like soil
- Water
- Nutrition
- Light
- A suitable temperature

Ultimately, if you get these things right, your plants are going to thrive. Let's take a quick look at them all in turn.

GROWING MEDIUM

A growing medium is simply the material in which a plant develops its roots. While soil is the default here, you can also grow things in non-soil media and in water.

The growing medium is simply there to allow the plant to access its water and nutrient needs. It might be composed of a single ingredient or a blend of several components.

We're first going to look at acquiring the ideal soil, to give you a solid base to work with, then we'll talk about some of the other options you might want to experiment with down the line.

SOIL

At first glance, soil looks very simple. It's just dirt, right? Well, actually, soil is so complex that there is an entire academic discipline, pedology, dedicated to its study. So there is a science in getting the soil right to best support your plants, but don't let that put you off, as the principles behind it are really straightforward.

Soil is made up of rotted organic material, together with minerals, water, gases and organisms. If you buy a bag of multipurpose compost from the garden centre, it will most likely contain a mix of moist, rotted organic material, but will lack the mineral component and the organisms of garden soil. That means it's still fine for some uses, but sometimes you might fare better if you add other stuff to it.

In particular, the mineral component is what gives soil most of its structure, which provides aeration and drainage to plant roots, functions that can be especially important for some plants and at certain stages of a plant's life.

So would it be better to grab some soil from outdoors instead? Well, no. While a lot of the organisms in outdoor soil are beneficial, there're also likely to be pests and diseases in there that you don't want to bring inside, especially where vulnerable young plants are concerned.

Instead, you can do one of three things. You can buy commercial mixes that are appropriate to what you are growing; you can buy regular, multipurpose compost and add non-soil media yourself; or you can make your own compost and modify that to make an ideal soil. For now, let's go with the simplest option of buying commercial mixes. Later on the book, we'll come back to the fun of making your own compost and blending your own soils.

For seedlings or mature plants that you bought or grew yourself, multipurpose compost or a potting mix is generally fine when you are looking to pot those plants on into containers. However, for growing from seed, multipurpose compost tends to be a little coarse and dries out quickly, so it's worthwhile buying a specially formulated seed mix. Alternatively, you can use a loam-based mix like John Innes. Loam is soil that is rich in organic matter with a good drainage balance between the two extremes of sand and clay.

You may also find composts that are specifically designed to be nutrient-rich for growing vegetables. These can be a great alternative to multipurpose for potting on, but again may not be the most suited to growing seeds. A fine, even soil surface and good drainage are what a seed is looking for. It doesn't need nutrition for germination, and too much nutrition early on can be a bad thing for crop performance.

It's understandable that the range of different compost and soil types on offer can be pretty confusing, but if you stick to a seed mix for growing seeds and multipurpose or potting compost for planting established seedlings into containers, you can't go far wrong in terms of growing medium!

WATER

Plants can be grown directly in water, without any need for soil. This technique is called hydroponics. Nutrients are dissolved in the water so the plant can get its water and nutrient needs in one go, meaning that the water itself is the growing medium.

There are various approaches to setting up hydroponic systems, the simplest of which is the floating raft method. Here, a sheet of foam is floated on the surface of water in a container. There are holes in the foam, into which net pots sit as porous containers for the plants. Nutrients are added to the water, and sometimes a pump is also used to circulate and oxygenate the water. Generally, quick-growing vegetables like lettuce are fine without the pump, but plants that take longer to grow do need that circulation.

There are also some great hydroponic kits you can buy which have the containers already set up, and which may also provide the light and heat that can help your plants really thrive. We will take a closer look at these systems later in the book. But before you go looking at buying fancy kits, how about some fun hydroponics projects you can set up for virtually no cost?

PROJECT: REGROW HERBS AND VEG

Regrow Herbs!

Herbs are a fantastic addition to any kitchen windowsill. Many herbs grow well in water – all you need is a glass, pot, or even an old plastic bottle and a herb plant from the store. You can then take cuttings from the parent plant and stand them in your container with some water. Spring water works best here, as it lacks the impurities of tap water and also contains trace elements that can help to feed the plant.

When you take your cuttings, just use a clean pair of scissors and make your cut just above a leaf. Roots will then grow a few weeks later from the "node" where the leaf used to be. Aim for healthy stems without a flower and take a piece about four or so inches (10cm) long. Strip off lower leaves so you just have the top third left. Change the water once a week once they've rooted and you'll have a ready supply of culinary herbs!

Herbs that are well suited to growing in water include:

- Mint
- Basil

- Oregano
- Sage
- Rosemary (soft, spring shoots work best)
- Thyme (again, best done in spring)
- Lemon balm

Regrow Veg!

Another fun experiment you may have heard of involves regrowing vegetable scraps in water. Again, this is super simple to do and is a great one for the kids. Container wise, a shallow bowl generally works best here. As with herbs, spring water is best and should be changed regularly.

Here are some easy veg to try regrowing:

- Celery – use the base and a couple of inches of the stems
- Lettuce – use the bottom few inches of any head-forming lettuce
- Fennel – use an inch or two of the base
- Spring/green onions – re-sprout the white base.
- Leeks – use a few inches of the base
- Garlic greens – use an old, whole garlic bulb that is starting to sprout, half submerge it and enjoy the fresh greens
- Carrot greens – save the tops of carrots and use the sprouting greens as you would parsley, or make a pesto

Regrow celery in water

WATER

You know that plants need water to thrive, but perhaps the most important thing to note here is that you can kill them with kindness. Particularly when growing in containers, overwatering your beloved plants is just as likely to bring about their demise as neglecting them altogether. The key is only to water when you actually need to.

The amount of water a plant needs depends on the type of plant, the stage of life it's in, and the medium it's growing in, as well as environmental factors like heat and humidity.

Adequate drainage is also important, and something we will talk about later.

If in doubt about whether or not a plant needs water, stick a finger into the soil up to at least the second knuckle (1.5–2" deep) and if your fingertip feels dry soil, water is needed.

It's better to water well when needed, so water begins to run out of the drainage holes in the container, rather than watering little and often. This is because the water can reach all of the roots and the plant is encouraged to root deeply.

However, in hot weather, you may still need to check the moisture in your containers twice a day.

Water the soil, not the plant itself. Wetting the foliage means that less of the water reaches the roots where it is needed and the risk of fungal infections increases.

NUTRITION

As well as a growing medium and water, plants need nutrients to thrive. The "big three" are nitrogen (N), phosphorous (P) and potassium (K). Nitrogen supports the above-ground growth of leaves, stems, branches and so on; phosphorous takes care of the below-ground growth of roots; and potassium feeds flowers and fruit. The old gardeners' rhyme for remembering the roles of NPK is "shoots, roots and fruits". Plants also need smaller amounts of trace elements such as magnesium and calcium.

Even if you use a growing medium that contains nutrition, like compost, eventually those nutrients will be depleted as they are used by the plants or washed away. We can therefore add fertiliser to keep the nutrient levels topped up.

You can buy slow-release fertilisers in pellet form to add to your compost mix when planting up containers, which will help to ensure that further nutrition is made steadily available throughout a growing season.

Liquid fertilisers are also a great option for fruit, vegetables and herbs, and they typically come in a highly concentrated form to be diluted for use, so one bottle goes a long way. I personally use an organic liquid seaweed fertiliser, which is inexpensive and offers a good balance of nutrients. Be sure to follow the instructions on the bottle when diluting the feed to the correct concentration for use, and don't be tempted to mix it stronger than it says.

As a general rule, aim to fertilise your veggies and herbs about once a month. The main exception is that fruiting plants need feeding more often when they are flowering and fruiting. I say "fruiting" plants rather than just "fruit", because this not only applies to fruit trees and bushes, but also to tomatoes, aubergines (eggplants), chillies, courgettes (zucchini) and anything else that produces a fruiting body. From the time that these plants begin to flower through to when you are harvesting, aim to fertilise once a week. The rest of the time, once a month is fine. For these fruiting plants, a liquid seaweed or anything advertised as a tomato feed will be fine, having the required levels of potassium to support the flowers and subsequent fruit.

LIGHT

You likely remember from school that plants need light in order to meet their energy requirements through photosynthesis. When planting outdoors, gardeners have to consider things like the amount of shade and the aspects of slopes to ensure each plant gets the light it needs. When it comes to apartment gardening, whether indoors or using exterior spaces like balconies and window boxes, light remains a central consideration.

If you are lucky enough to have a balcony that faces south, your light levels should be great and you should be blessed with lots of sunny growing conditions in the summer. Otherwise, you will be dealing with at least partial shade and that might affect what you choose to grow. Sun-loving veg like aubergines (eggplants) and tomatoes are likely to struggle in shade, but leafy greens like kale, spinach and rocket (arugula) will thrive. The same applies to window-boxes.

When growing indoors, windowsills are our friends. But again, a south-facing windowsill will receive more light from the sun. This doesn't necessarily mean it is better for all edibles, especially in summer, when the heat of a south-facing windowsill can be too intense for some plants. The old gardening adage of "right plant, right place" applies indoors just as much as it does outdoors. That said, a broad range of veg and herbs will be perfectly happy on a south-facing windowsill through the spring and summer months, so this is a prime growing spot for the apartment gardener.

So how much light is enough light? For most veg and herbs, fourteen to sixteen hours of light is needed, six to eight hours of which should be in direct sun. There are outliers on either side of this average, so if you have windowsills or other areas with significantly more or less sunlight or direct sun, you can still find the perfect plants to grow there.

Specifically, if you only have around twelve hours of moderate light a day, you can still grow:

- Spinach
- Rocket (arugula)
- Leafy salad (corn salad (mache); lettuce that does not form a head)
- Oriental greens (mizuna and mibuna (mustard greens))
- Kale
- Swiss chard
- Peas
- Radishes
- Watercress
- Sorrel
- Microgreens

If, on the other hand, you are seeing upwards of fourteen hours of full, direct sun, you are more likely to see success with some of the trickier plants, namely:

- Tomatoes
- Aubergines (eggplants)

- Sweet peppers (capsicums)
- Strawberries
- Citrus

If the climate where you live, the layout of your apartment, or the season (autumn/fall, winter) mean that your plants are unlikely to get enough light over a long enough period of the day, you have the option to buy grow lights. We will talk more about choosing appropriate grow lights later in the book.

TEMPERATURE

Temperature affects the ability of seeds to germinate, the rate at which plants grow and sometimes their ability to fruit, as well as ultimately their prospects of survival.

Most plants are adapted to deal with some level of temperature fluctuation, but each cultivar has thresholds of high and low temperatures past which it will not thrive and thresholds past which it is likely to die. The good news is that as an apartment or indoor gardener, you get to exert quite a lot of control over the temperatures your plants are exposed to. Similar to the case with light, you can exert this control both by choosing the best spot for each plant and in some instances by providing an additional heat source.

GROWING FROM SEED

Temperature is also important when it comes to growing plants from seed. Most seeds won't germinate (sprout) at temperatures below about 7°C (45°F), which thankfully isn't an issue for us indoor growers, as room temperature tends to fall in the range of 15-25° Celsius. Warmer temperatures usually mean better germination, and the ideal germination temperatures for veg seeds generally fall in the range of 18-30°C (65-85°F).

However, we should take into account that the best spots for germinating seeds are on our windowsills, due to the light availability, but windowsills can be warmer than the rest of the room on sunny, summer days, and cooler in winter. We might therefore have to be a little bit careful of overheating seeds and seedlings on those very hot days, but more critically, we might want to provide an extra helping hand to seeds sown in the winter months.

A basic "propagator" consists simply of a tray with a clear, ventilated lid, and can help to keep heat and moisture contained while seeds are germinating. They are inexpensive and can really speed things along in the cooler months. Propagators with heated bases or heat mats for propagators are also available, and are especially useful for veg that prefer a little more heat to get going. I use a windowsill heated propagator to start my tomato and chilli seedlings in January, for example. We'll come back to these later in the book.

A basic propagator

GROWING ON

Once seedlings are established and you have moved them to containers to grow on into mature plants (we'll talk about how to do that later), temperature will still affect how well they grow. Vegetables and herbs can be loosely divided into "warm season" and "cool season" crops, which helps us to understand their ideal temperature ranges.

Warm season crops may potentially be grown year round indoors, if your ambient room temperatures remain high enough or you provide an additional heat source like a heated grow mat. Avoid using fan heaters, as they will dry plants out too quickly, and most plants hate draughts. In summer, you may be able to grow warm season crops outdoors on a balcony or in window boxes, if the temperatures of your region and site allow. You can check the temperature of the areas you are looking to use for germination or growing on using a basic thermometer.

Most warm season veg and herbs are looking for daytime temperatures of around 27°C (80°F) and nighttime temperatures of around 17°C (63°F) as an ideal. You can get away with lower temperatures, but they will grow less quickly and the lower the temperature drops, the more likely it is that these plants will either be prevented from fruiting or stop growing entirely.

Warm season plants include the following:

Veg:

- Tomatoes
- Lima, mung, soy and green beans (French; runner; snap)
- Aubergines (eggplants)
- Squash
- Chillies

- Sweet peppers (capsicum)
- Sweet potatoes
- Mustard

Herbs:

- Basil
- Coriander (cilantro)
- Marjoram
- French tarragon
- Chervil

There is a lot of variation between cultivars, so do read up on the specific varieties you are looking to grow if you want to be more precise here. For example, some popular tomato varieties like "Moneymaker" and "Gardeners' Delight" are bred for outdoor summer growing and can handle more temperature variance, whereas others are fussier about consistent warmth. If you are concerned about only having a short seasonal window of warmth and sunlight, you might opt for more compact varieties, such as dwarf aubergines (eggplants) and cherry tomatoes.

Cool season crops are generally more forgiving, so many of these will be our go-to plants for apartment gardening throughout much of the year. We are looking for daytime temperatures within the broad range of 10-21°C (50-70°F) and ideally night temperatures that drop to 7-12°C (45-55°F), although in most cases it doesn't matter if these plants stay a little warmer at night. We do have to be careful with some of these – notably spinach, radishes and rocket (arugula) – in the height of summer, as hotter temperatures can induce bolting (wherein the plants set seed), which spoils the crop. But in general, these veg and herbs are pretty easy to grow.

Cool season plants include the following:

Veg:

- Swiss chard
- Beets
- Cress
- Kale
- Broad beans
- Chicory
- Lettuce
- Carrots
- Onions
- Shallots
- Radishes
- Spinach
- Sorrel
- Kohlrabi
- Broccoli
- Celery
- Potatoes

Herbs:

- Parsley
- Mint
- Rosemary
- Thyme
- Sage
- Oregano
- Chives
- Dill

When it comes to growing fruit, citrus trees, figs and strawberries should all be happy with a temperature that stays above around 15°C (60°F) during their fruiting season. Certain types are better suited for indoor growing, and we will look at these later on. Strawberries are hardy so are fine with cold over the winter if you have them in outdoor areas, but citrus and figs will typically prefer to be brought indoors over the colder months if you've been keeping them out on a balcony in summer. If you're looking to get a little more exotic and grow bananas, avocados or pineapples, they prefer warmer temperatures of 21°C (70°F) or higher.

᪣

We've now covered the basic ingredients your plants will need to thrive: a growing medium, water, nutrition, light and a suitable temperature. Don't worry if you haven't absorbed all of the specifics yet; you can come back to this section and we will also talk about specific plants in more detail later in the book. We can get things rolling now with something practical.

In the next chapter, we'll take a look at the equipment you may need, then talk about getting started with growing from seed!

CHAPTER 2

GETTING STARTED

Now we've dealt with some of the key theory behind keeping your plants healthy and productive, let's move on without further ado to the practical business of growing.

In this chapter, we'll look at the basic equipment you need to get started, plus a few optional extras that may come in handy. Then I'll take you, step by step, through the simple process of growing from seed. Finally, we'll think about some of the practicalities and potential when growing in containers, then wrap up with a fun upcycling project.

APARTMENT GARDENING GEAR

As with many hobbies, the list of equipment and extras you could buy for your apartment kitchen garden is very long indeed. You could acquire enough kit to make your apartment resemble a futuristic lab, filled with pristine, white cabinets of lush, hydroponic greens under grow lights and showcasing tropical specimens in misted chambers. Or you could just have a few free herb cuttings in recycled yoghurt pots on your kitchen windowsill. The sky's the limit, but you certainly don't need a lot of expensive equipment to get started!

First we'll look at basic equipment you will find useful to start you off. Then we'll consider some of the optional stuff that you might want to splash out on in time, if you want to increase your yields and growing season or perhaps support a wider range of edibles.

BASIC EQUIPMENT

Even in the case of the basics, there are often alternatives to buying new, specialist items from the store. You can improvise and perhaps recycle things you already have at hand. I really like recycling and upcycling in my gardening, to reduce waste and costs but also to be creative, and we're going to look later on in the book at some great projects you can try to make your own upcycled containers.

Even when it comes to acquiring seed, you don't always necessarily have to buy it in little packets; you can save seed from a wide variety of supermarket vegetables. I've had great success growing chillies, tomatoes, and squash from the seeds of store-bought produce, and often grow pea shoots from cheap, dried, supermarket peas. And we've already seen how you can make new herb plants by taking cuttings from store-bought herb pots.

The only things I'd suggest you really have to buy are a good growing medium – and even there you can save money by mixing your own medium rather than buying ready-mixed specialist bags of seed or potting compost – plus fertiliser, if you're growing anything that is not very quick to mature.

Let's have a look at other basic equipment and ways in which you can improvise:

- Growing medium – multipurpose compost will do for potting on and for sowing larger seeds; a seed compost is ideal for finer seeds in particular. Alternatively, you could leave out the soil and get a hydroponics kit.
- Seed trays and/or pots for seedlings – here you can repurpose mushroom and tomato punnets and yoghurt pots. Remember to make drainage holes in the base.
- Small trowel or scoop for filling pots and trays. You could make your own by cutting a section out of a plastic milk carton.
- Small dibber for making holes for seedlings – you

can substitute the back of a pen or even your finger.
- Containers for mature plants – these can be shop-bought pots or may be repurposed from the bottom sections of drinks bottles. We'll look at how to make them look interesting later in the book.
- Small watering can or spray bottle – here you can use a plastic milk carton with small holes poked in the lid for pouring, if you wish.
- Saucers or trays to put underneath containers – to catch any water that runs out of drainage holes. You can substitute here with an old plate, bowl or any watertight container.
- Fertiliser – a general liquid feed like an organic seaweed feed is perhaps the most versatile option. You can also get slow-release fertiliser pellets to mix in with compost when planting.

Water with a small watering can with a fine rose, a spray bottle or a repurposed milk carton

OPTIONAL EQUIPMENT

Depending on what you are growing and in what area of your apartment, you may also benefit from a few extras. Most of these are inexpensive to buy.

- Thermometer – for checking the temperature of different areas are suitable for the plants you intend to grow there.
- Plant labels – useful for remembering which plants and seedlings are which. You can buy plastic, wooden or even reusable slate ones, or simply save your wooden ice cream sticks and use those!
- Plant supports and twine – taller and more ungainly plants like kale, peppers, tomatoes and broccoli might benefit from a stick support pushed into the soil. Wooden flower sticks or small garden canes are fine here. Use soft twine to tie them in loosely, not wire, which may damage stems. Alternatively, an old allotment trick I was taught is to cut up an old pair of women's tights into bands, which make ideal, soft, flexible ties.
- Vertical growing aids – particularly for making the most of balcony walls, trellis can be a good option for growing climbers like cucumbers, some squash or even passionfruit. There are also a variety of growing pouches and modular units for sale for both indoor and outdoor use so you can create "green walls" of growing produce.

If you have a little more budget to spend and are looking for some more advanced gear to help your apartment kitchen garden along, you might also consider the following:

- Grow lights – to extend to growing season or expand the areas of your apartment suited to growing.
- Heat mats and heated propagators – to provide extra warmth to seeds and plants that need it.
- Hydroponic kits – to get into soil-less growing with minimal setup.

We will talk about what to look for in this additional gear later in the book. For now, let's stick to the basics and get our hands dirty!

STARTING FROM SEED

It's easy to sow seeds indoors. All you need are seeds, a container and a suitable growing medium like a seed compost mix. For the container, a seed tray, small pots or a propagator all work, but if you don't have any purpose-made containers, you can use yoghurt pots with a hole poked in the bottom, or tomato or mushroom punnets. All that matters is that the container can hold compost and drain freely.

If you can't get seed compost, multipurpose compost will be okay for most seeds, unless they are very small. You can also make your own seed mix, which we will deal with a little later.

The only other equipment you need is a small watering can with a fine rose (sprinkler head with fine holes) or a spray bottle.

The simple steps to sowing seeds are as follows:

1. Fill the container with compost, then either take it to the sink or place it inside a larger bowl that can catch water.
2. Use the spray bottle or watering can to thoroughly wet the compost, then allow it to drain.

3. Sprinkle seeds evenly over the surface of the compost (except in the case of very large seeds like squash seeds, which can be individually placed). The seed packet may indicate ideal spacings; if not, aim for 2-3cm between each seed.
4. Cover the seeds with a very thin layer of compost (aim for the same thickness as the seeds themselves)
5. To help retain moisture and warmth, you can optionally cover the pot or tray at this point with clear plastic such as a transparent polythene bag or cling film; if using a propagator, put on the lid. Remove this plastic covering as soon as you see seedlings starting to emerge.

Once your seedlings have sprouted, you will need to leave them in situ until they develop their first pair of "true" leaves. This is the second set of leaves they grow, as they first produce an embryonic leaf or two with the cool name of "cotyledons". These will look markedly different to the true leaves, so you will easily be able to tell the difference.

Once that second pair of leaves, the true leaves, emerge, the seedlings are ready to be "pricked out" and potted on. You can opt to pot them on to a seed tray and space them 5cm (2") apart from one another to grow on for a couple of weeks, or else pop them individually straight into small (7.5–9cm/3-3.5") pots.

For potting on, the steps are as follows:

1. Prepare the seed tray or pots with multipurpose compost or a potting mix.
2. Lift out clumps of seedlings with your fingers or with the aid of a spoon and very loosely start to separate them out.
3. Handling seedlings only by the leaves (stems and

roots are very easily crushed) lift them out, one at a time.

4. Using a small dibber, your finger or the back of a pen, poke a hole in the growing medium large enough to drop a seedling in such that the roots are covered.

5. Lower the seedling into place, then shake the tray so the rest of the hole fills in around the seedling. Again, this avoids damaging the plant by pressing soil around by hand. (Note: it's okay if it flops over to begin with; it will right itself within a day or two). Repeat for the rest.

6. After a couple of weeks, the plants should be strong enough to move on to their final growing positions.

GROWING IN CONTAINERS

I want to round off this chapter with some general pointers about growing in containers throughout your apartment kitchen garden.

Because of the importance of good drainage, it's generally best to opt for containers with holes in the bottom. To catch any excess water that runs through, you can opt to put a tray or saucer underneath, or, failing that, sit them on an old tea towel or some kitchen paper.

There is a wide range of containers available, with pots and troughs in different shapes and sizes, made of plastic, metal, ceramic or wood. You may find decorative ceramic pots, designed for houseplants, that don't come with holes; you can absolutely use these, but treat them as a decorative outer with a drainable pot inside. You may wish to elevate the inner pot slightly with something like a stone or a trimmed down section of a yoghurt pot so there is a good drainage gap.

If buying plastic, a greener choice is to opt for a recycled pot or, failing that, just to avoid black plastic, which is not currently widely recyclable. Alternatively, you can make your own plastic container from an old yoghurt pot or drinks bottle as a funky upcycling project!

PROJECT: UPCYCLED BOTTLE POTS

Make and decorate your own pots using old bottles

1. Keep an empty plastic drinks bottle. A large milk bottle or a 2l soft drink bottle is ideal. You can also use cardboard drinks cartons.
2. Mark a line all the way around at your desired height and cut away the top, so you are left with the open, lower section of the bottle.
3. Trim off any sharp bits so the finish is smooth and safe. You can use a little sandpaper if you think it needs it.
4. Paint on a design with acrylic or poster paints. Animal faces can work well, or you could just go freestyle with colours and patterns.
5. For drainage, either carefully poke a few holes in the base with a biro or small knife, or sit another, drainable pot inside, slightly elevated.
6. Pot up with veg, herbs, or perhaps a strawberry plant, and enjoy!

Get creative! For an animal planter with a difference, you could shape out some little ears when cutting out, or perhaps even incorporate a milk carton's handle as a nose or elephant's trunk. So many possibilities!

A quirky pig pot made from a plastic bottle

Now you're up to scratch with all the basics, from the fundamentals of what your plants need to thrive, to the basic equipment you need, to the practicalities of growing and planting your plants. In the next part of the book, we'll look at the kinds of plants you might what to choose for your apartment or indoor kitchen garden.

PART II
CHOOSING YOUR PLANTS

With the essential principles and practicalities of growing tucked firmly into your belt, you can start to think about what you actually want to grow and what is suitable for your situation.

Depending on where you live, not all vegetables, fruit, herbs and other edibles might be best suited to your growing conditions in terms of light and temperature, although as we learned in the last chapter, there is equipment available such as grow lights that can broaden the range of options.

The other key restriction for growing in and around an apartment is space. We are going to be growing in containers of one form or another, which restricts the amount of room available for plants' roots. Some plants also take up a lot of space when they are mature, meaning there can be physical limitations on what you can fit into a given area. All of this being said, there are still plenty of plants that are ideal for your apartment or indoor garden. You'll be harvesting all sorts of tasty goodies from your own verdant little productive oasis in no time!

In this section, we're going to look at a selection of vegetables, herbs, fruits, as well as a few other, more unusual edibles, together with the growing conditions they each need to thrive. Why not start noting down some of the plants you might want to try growing as you read through?

CHAPTER 3

VEGETABLES

As you may remember from Chapter 1, vegetables can be loosely categorised into warm season and cool season veg. When growing outside, that generally means warm season veg are summer crops and cool season veg are suited to other times of the year. When growing indoors, the light requirements of most warm season crops means they are still best grown in summer unless using grow lights, despite the fact it is warmer indoors than outdoors through the other seasons. However, we do have access to a longer growing window for a lot of the cool season crops, many of which can be grown year round indoors.

We'll take a tour of some of the broad range of cool season veg first, then move on to the smaller group of warm season veg. The plants are tackled in alphabetical order to make this chapter easy to refer back to for reference.

COOL SEASON VEG

BEETROOT

Beets are really easy to grow, don't take up much space, and are ready to eat a couple of months after sowing. While it is possible to sow into plugs or a seed tray, beets are like most root veg in that they are easily disturbed upon potting on, so it's better to sow direct into their final container if you can. Pop the seeds in at least four inches (10cm) apart, unless growing baby beets.

Opt for round varieties, rather than cylindrical or tapering varieties, when growing in a container. Beets have a long tap root, so like a few inches of space below the main body of the vegetable. A container six to ten inches (15-25cm) deep should be fine for most varieties.

If you sow some every few weeks, you can have a supply to take you through much of the year. They're fine with cool temperatures but do like a good amount of light. Keep the compost moist but not sodden.

Start harvesting when they're around the size of a golf ball (1.5"/4cm+) and don't let them get bigger than a cricket ball (2.5"/6.5cm) in diameter or they will become tough. You can also eat the leaves, sautéed until lightly wilted, like spinach.

"Boltardy" is a reliable variety that I grow every year without issue, and as the name suggests, it is resistant to running to seed (bolting) if conditions get a bit warmer and drier. Another great cultivar for indoor growing is "Pablo", which is great harvested young as baby beets, so you need less space and can get your harvest more quickly.

BROAD BEANS

Outdoor kitchen gardeners often sow their broad beans indoors in autumn or winter to give them a head start before planting them out once the ground has warmed. However, if you have a sunny spot in your apartment or on a balcony to situate a large container, you can still grow them to maturity. Each plant needs about a foot (30cm) in width and depth, so you could use individual 30cm pots or a trough for several plants.

You can sow broad beans directly to their containers by dibbing a hole a couple of inches deep, pushing in a seed and covering. However, for best germination, I'd recommend starting them on a windowsill first, then planting them on after about six weeks. Broad beans have deep roots, so either sow them individually in small pots, use root trainers (plastic moulds to support deep roots), or, like me, you could use toilet roll tubes. I save the cardboard tubes then arrange them to fill a seed tray (with the holes facing up), fill them with compost then sow a seed into each one. When it comes to planting on, just sink the plant into its new home with the tube still attached – it will degrade naturally over time.

Once they are planted on, they may need the support of a cane to stop them falling over as they grow taller. Always keep them well watered. Once you see the first pods forming on the lowest truss, pinch out the tops of the plants to encourage fruiting. You can also give them some liquid feed at this point if you wish. Those pinched out tops are delicious in stir fries. In fact, if you don't have room for mature broad beans, you can still grow them to eat as sautéed shoots.

You can either harvest pods when they are about three inches (8cm) long and cook them whole or wait until you can see the beans protruding through the pod to pick them and shell them.

I'd recommend a dwarf variety like "The Sutton" for the best results with container growing. They only reach about a foot and a half (45cm) in height. If you have a big balcony trough or larger pot, you might try "Masterpiece Green Longpod" for a bigger plant with lots of beans.

BROCCOLI

The big round heads of broccoli you get in the supermarket are a type of broccoli called calabrese. While you can grow these if you like, from experience I don't think they're as good as sprouting broccoli varieties, both in terms of the amount of crop you get from a small space and also flavour. Sprouting cultivars come in both white and purple options and they throw out lots of individual spears of broccoli which are delicious steamed, roasted or stir fried.

To grow indoors, you can potentially start sprouting broccoli off at any time of year. It's tolerant of cold and can take a bit of shade, although like most plants will grow faster in warmth and light. Aside from consistent watering, the only real thing to keep an eye on with these plants is that they want to flower and go to seed when it gets hot, so you'll want to pick them as soon as they're ready, especially in the warmer months. What you are harvesting is actually the immature flower buds, so if you leave them on the plant too long, you'll end up with a mass of yellow flowers followed by seeds.

To harvest, cut sprouting stems once you see the purple or white head is formed. The plant will then continue to throw out further stems, so you get an ongoing crop for a month or more. Neat!

CARROTS

As you might expect, carrots generally need a container that's quite deep (8-12") so that their long root can burrow down. However, there are some compact chantenay and ball varieties that are superb for shallower containers, and you can harvest any variety young as sweet, baby carrots.

Carrots are also especially keen on a light, free-draining soil, so if you have a bit of extra grit or vermiculite to mix in to the growing medium, they'll do all the better (see the later section on compost mixes).

Some carrot varieties: left to right, Royal Chantenay; Little Finger; Rondo

Like beets, carrots are best sown in situ. The seeds are quite small, so rather than placing them individually, you can sprinkle them very thinly across the surface and cover with a light layer of compost. Once they have germinated, you can then thin them out so the remainder are two to three inches (5-8cm) apart.

If you sow some every few weeks, you can harvest through much of the year. Most varieties mature in around 70 days, but pick them at whatever size you like.

"Chantenay Red Cored" is a solid choice for indoor growing, reaching no more than about five inches at maturity but having a sweet and juicy flavour and a reddish centre. "Royal Chantenay" is a similar, slightly rounder variety that crops reliably. In smaller containers, "Little Finger" are ideal for their three- to four-inch length, or you could opt for one of the many round carrot varieties, such as "Rondo" or "Paris Market 5".

CELERY

Celery is a bog plant, so it likes plenty of water. For this reason, it's a great choice for hydroponic growing. If you're growing it in soil, it's especially important with this plant that it never dries out. Although a cool season crop, it doesn't like to fall below 10°C (50°F) or it will run to seed, so it works well for indoor growing.

Plants can be sown in situ or transplanted into position. You'll need a container that is at least eight inches (20cm) deep and six to eight inches (15-20cm) wide per plant, or else use the same spacings in a trough.

As well as being thirsty, celery is quite a hungry crop and will thank you for a liquid feed once a fortnight. Harvest once the celery is the desired size.

Choose a self-blanching variety, which means you won't have to bury the stems to keep them white. "Tango" grows quickly and matures with slightly shorter stems than other varieties, so is a good choice for a container. "Loretta" is another reliable cultivar that was bred for reduced stringiness and a sweet flavour.

CHICORY

Leaf chicory actually comes in three distinct cultivated types. You may be most familiar with the "non-forcing" or "sugar loaf" types that form a large, hearted head similar to a lettuce. Then there are the red "radicchio" varieties. The third category contains the "forcing" types (also known as "witloof" and "Belgian endive") the roots of which are lifted from the ground and forced in cool and dark conditions to form a pale, dense head ("chicon"). Forcing types take extra work and tend to do best when grown outside then forced indoors, so we'll just talk about the former two types here.

Within these categories there are a wide range of cultivars to experiment with. All of the types can be eaten raw in salads or cooked, although smaller leaves are generally chosen for salads, as they are less bitter than older leaves. You can also sow non-forcing and radicchio types year round indoors for baby leaves.

You can sow right into containers or transplant from a seed tray. Mature plants want to be at least eight inches (20cm) apart, but for baby leaves you can sow them more densely and just cut some when you want to use them. Baby leaves should only take a month or so to grow.

Keep soil moist and feed once a fortnight if you are hoping for a mature head. Once the head has formed, harvest by cutting cleanly at the base and leave the root in the ground to resprout small leaves.

"Pan di Zucchero" is a sugar loaf variety that performs well for forming hearts. "Variegato di Castelfranco" has attractive, bicoloured leaves and is great both for harvesting young or allowing to mature. It looks fantastic in salads, especially when mixed in with some juicy red radicchio, like "Palla Rossa".

By the way, if you grow a radicchio type and it does not turn red, put it somewhere cool for a couple of weeks and it should encourage the reddening of the leaves.

CRESS AND WATERCRESS

Cress is probably the easiest veg to grow, and is a great one to try with kids. You can sow cress seeds any time of year on a tray lined with damp tissue or cotton wool and they will quickly sprout on a windowsill. If you cover the tray with cling/wrapping film until they germinate, it will help to keep the moisture in. You can also use a spray bottle to give them a spritz.

Alternatively, you can sow them onto a seed mix in a tray or pot. The added nutrients should mean you get to cut and regrow the cress more times before the plants are exhausted. For a fun project with kids, you could come up with some novelty containers like old eggshells or yoghurt pots with faces drawn on.

Harvest cress by trimming with scissors when it reaches an inch or more in height, then leave it to regrow.

You might encounter curled, Greek or common varieties, which all have a mustardy flavour but with different intensities and textures, so you can experiment to find the balance you like. "Extra curled" is a popular and fairly mild variety with very curly leaves.

Watercress is actually a different species to regular cress. All cress likes moist conditions, but as the name suggests, watercress depends on things being very damp and unsurprisingly it is a great choice for hydroponic growing. I've had success growing it very simply in a large bowl of water and just letting its roots sprawl while I trimmed the shoots to eat – delicious! If you are going to try this, just be sure to change the water at least once a week to stop it going stagnant.

LETTUCE

There's a really wide variety of lettuce available, with different forms, colours and textures. Some are loose-leaf types and others form hearts. They're all straightforward to grow, but for your apartment garden, I'd most recommend the cut-and-come-again types. As the name suggests, these are loose-leaf lettuces that you cut while relatively young and they will resprout for a second (and perhaps even a third) cropping. Many seed companies sell these in attractive mixes and you can be cropping them in as little as four to six weeks from sowing!

A typical cut-and-come-again lettuce mix

You can thinly scatter seeds in a tray, pot or trough and just thin them out later, transplanting thinnings to other containers if you wish. Cover the tiny seeds with a very thin layer of compost. Cut-and-come-again lettuces can be placed as close as three or four inches (8-10cm) apart, while mature loose-leaf and head varieties will need at least six inches (15cm) each – check the seed packet for the variety you buy.

"Salad Bowl" is a nice multicoloured cut-and-come-again

mix, but most seed companies do their own version. "Little Gem" is a sweet and crunchy head type with a compact heart.

MICROGREENS

These have become more popular in recent years, hailed for their excellent nutritional concentrations. Microgreens are simply the young sprouted seedlings of a variety of crops. Popular plants for microgreens include radish, kale, coriander, amaranth and peas. They are incredibly easy and quick to grow, and their ease combined with the sheer variety of colours and forms open to you make microgreens another fun option to grow with kids, or for your own pleasure!

They can be grown in a tray, pots or troughs and also work very well as hydroponic veg. There are microgreen kits available that involve a tray and some capillary matting to act as a growing medium for the roots for a simple hydroponic arrangement.

Pea shoots are probably my favourite microgreens, and they can be grown so easily and cheaply. Simply buy a bag of dried peas from the supermarket, leave some to soak overnight in water, then scatter them over a tray of soil. You don't even need to bury them – just water and wait for the magic to start happening within days! You can then start harvesting within a week or two by cutting them off at the base as you need them.

You can find specialist microgreens seed mixes, but you can also try a wide variety of crops yourself. For a bit of colour, try red-stemmed radishes, "Bulls Blood" beetroots, and amaranth. Leafy herbs like coriander, fenugreek, basil and parsley also work well. Other great options include sunflowers, broccoli and rocket (arugula).

ONIONS AND SHALLOTS

Onions and shallots can either be grown from seed or from "sets", which are immature bulbs. You can also buy young plants from the garden centre. Because of the time and space required, I don't think regular onions are really worth growing in an apartment. However, shallots and spring onions (scallions) are more space efficient.

Spring onions can be sown quite densely in a tray or pot, then transplanted to spacings a couple of inches apart. They also make good filler plants to dot around other crops in mixed containers or window boxes. Harvest from when the stem is pencil thickness.

Shallots can be grown from seed, but it's quicker and easier here to opt for sets. A set will also produce a cluster of bulbs, whereas each seed will only produce one bulb. You can get round varieties and elongated, so-called banana varieties. Plant sets by pushing into the compost so the tip is just showing, at spacings of six to eight inches (15-20cm). Harvest once the foliage yellows and begins to topple.

Shallots and onions do like a sunny spot. They need to be well watered, but good drainage is especially important here, as they are prone to fungal diseases. You can grow spring onions year round in the right conditions, but shallots will likely perform best if planted in spring.

"White Lisbon" is the best known spring onion and it is reliable and easy to grow. For something a little different, "Rossa Lunga di Firenze" is an Italian cultivar of red onion that looks and tastes great! You can harvest them young as spring onions or let the elongated bulbs mature and try roasting them whole.

"Longor" is a pointy, banana-type shallot with a great flavour that will give you up to eight bulbs per set. "Meloine" is likewise a heavy producer, but produces flattened rounded forms with a reddish tinge.

POTATOES

Potatoes can grow well in large containers, which means they are suitable for an apartment or indoor garden if you have a bit of space for a big pot (at least 40 l), tub or potato growing bag (available from garden centres).

You can try planting supermarket potatoes if you want, but the special seed potatoes you'll find at garden centres are certified virus free and you'll have a bigger range to choose from. Before planting, "chit" the potatoes by laying them out on a light windowsill for a few weeks to sprout. There is an old gardeners' trick of placing them in empty egg boxes to keep them nicely spaced and aerated, which is something I've always done too.

Start with about four inches (10cm) of compost in your container, then space out three to five of your chitted potatoes on top. Bury them with another four or so inches of compost. Once the shoots have grown four inches above the surface, bury them, and repeat that process until your pot is full. When the flowers open on the plant, the potatoes should be ready! They should be about the size of a hen's egg on average. The entire process from planting to harvest should take seventy to ninety days.

Choose a first or second early variety, which are smaller and faster growing, making them better suited to containers than maincrop potatoes. "Swift" is a fast growing early potato with round tubers with white flesh and skin. "Kestrel" produces pale, oval tubers with bits of purple and is a good all-rounder in the kitchen. For something a little different, "Anya" has a very distinctive appearance with its long and knobbly tubers, and an equally distinctive nutty taste.

ROCKET (ARUGULA)

Rocket grows very well in containers and sowing a small amount every few weeks can supply you with leaves year round. If you like a strong peppery hit in your salads, you can let the leaves mature; alternatively, you can start harvesting baby leaves, which are milder and more tender, after about a month. Mature leaves can also be sautéed like spinach.

Sprinkle seeds in a tray or container of your choice, much as you would for cut-and-come-again lettuce. Keep the plants moist but not sodden. Rocket likes light, but protect it from the heat of intense, summer sun, else the leaves will become tough and the plant may more readily bolt. If and when flower buds do appear, either pinch them out to prolong cropping or let them flower and eat the flowers as a garnish!

With both sowing and harvesting, little and often is the way forward with rocket. Harvest a few leaves from each plant at a time, so it's not weakened too much and can continue to regrow tender leaves.

In terms of varieties, you can get both wild and various kinds of cultivated (salad) rocket. Wild rocket has a more intense flavour, while salad rockets, like "Runaway", tend to be faster growing. However, some cultivars, like "Skyrocket", have been bred to strike a balance of both attributes.

SPINACH

Spinach is another really handy crop that you can potentially keep going right through the year. Like rocket, small sowings every few weeks can keep you in a successional harvest.

Sow thinly in a tray or other container and either cut them as baby leaves or thin them to three-inch (8cm) spacings to mature. As the plants grow larger, you can then continue to harvest some and leave the rest with more room to grow.

You may see spinach varieties presented as summer or

winter varieties, but these distinctions matter more when growing outdoors. If growing spinach on a balcony or window box, sow summer varieties from mid-spring and throughout the summer, and sow winter varieties in autumn for a hardier crop that will be okay in the cold. Indoors, you can likely get away with summer varieties year round, along with anything labelled as an all-year-round variety. Just keep summer varieties away from intense sun in the height of summer – they do well with a little shade or on a windowsill that does not face south. On the flip side, if you are growing winter varieties in window boxes or on a balcony, they will thank you for a bright and sunny spot through the cooler months.

"Missouri" does well in containers and seems adaptable to different growing conditions, doing well in summer due to its tendency to bolt slowly. "Matador" is a reliable all-year-round variety with large, rich leaves. "Giant Winter" is a prolific winter variety with extra-large leaves and a great taste.

Alternatively, you can also get "perpetual spinach", which is actually chard, but for all intents and purposes can be used just like spinach. It's fully hardy outdoors, fine with indoor growing, and it's perennial, so it's an easy, catch-all option!

WARM SEASON VEG

The five warm season "veg" we're going to look at here are all actually not veg at all – they're fruit. We're not interested in eating the leaves, stems or roots of these plants; instead we're after the fruiting parts – parts that contain seeds and are produced from the flowers. As with most of the fruit we eat, these plants originate from warmer climes and in Europe and North America are treated as warm season crops.

That doesn't mean these plants are necessarily hard to grow, though; in fact, they should thrive under your care in the warmth of your apartment or indoor space!

AUBERGINES (EGGPLANTS)

Aubergines need sunshine and warmth to thrive. It's best to sow them right at the start of the year, so they come to maturity through the sunnier months, unless using artificial sources of light and heat.

Sow in small pots and leave them somewhere warm to germinate – they don't need light for germination, so an airing cupboard works well if you don't have a heated propagator –

but move them to a bright, warm windowsill once they have sprouted. As with many of these edibles, you can also opt to buy established plants from spring onwards. They'll need 9" (23cm) of room once established.

Support with a cane to stop them flopping, tying in the main stem, and pinch out the top shoot when they reach a foot (30cm) or so to encourage sideshoots and more flowers and fruit. Feed with a liquid seaweed or tomato feed weekly from when the flowers emerge.

Aubergines, like chillies and tomatoes, are technically self-pollinating, which means you don't need multiple plants in order to get them to fruit. Instead, pollen naturally moves from one flower of a plant to another flower by insects or simply being blown in the wind. However, when plants spend their lives indoors, you may need to give them a helping hand. Once flowers are fully formed, take a small artists' paintbrush or a cotton bud/swab and swirl it gently inside the flower, picking up tiny pollen. Then swirl it around in the centre of another flower to transfer it, and repeat with the remaining flowers. This should help to ensure that the plant sets fruit.

Misting your aubergine plants a couple of times a day with tepid water will encourage fruiting and also help to deter red spider mites, a common pest.

I've found better results from growing cultivars with many smaller fruits, rather than trying to grow huge ones, but you could experiment with some of the many types to see what works for you. If you do opt for a large-fruited variety, allow four to six flowers to form, then pinch out any others so the plant isn't overstretched and you have a better chance of decent fruits forming.

"Garline" and "Kaberi" both have a compact form that means they do great in containers; they produce a large number of small, glossy, fruit that look like little purple eggs. For something a little different, "Clara" produces fruit of medium size with pure white skins and flesh.

CHILLIES

Chillies are so fun to grow: they look and taste great and there are so many varieties to choose from. They are also perfect for containers, as they fruit better with slightly restricted roots.

The earlier in the year you sow your chillies, the earlier and longer your harvest can be. Seeds need some warmth to germinate, so a heated propagator is ideal, but they should still sprout fine indoors on a warm windowsill. Sow a couple of seeds per small pot to get them going, or sow very thinly in a seed tray. You can help them along by covering the pot with a clear plastic bag and securing with string or an elastic band. This both keeps heat in and raises the humidity, aiding germination. Take the bag off as soon as they start to spout.

Move them on once they hit an inch or so in height to pots of around eight inches (20cm) or a little more in diameter. Keep the soil moist but never waterlogged. A quick mist of the plants with a spray bottle once in a while will also help to provide chillies the humidity they prefer. Feed weekly with a liquid seaweed or tomato feed from when the flowers appear. You may need to support plants with a small cane or flower stick as they mature.

As with aubergines, you can help chillies to set fruit indoors by manually pollinating the flowers with a small paintbrush or cotton bud.

When it comes to harvesting chillies, you have a choice. You can pick them when they are green, which makes them milder than ripened fruit and will encourage further cropping. Or you can let them mature to their ripe colour (which may be red, orange, yellow, purple or black, depending on the variety) for a richer and hotter flavour.

There are hundreds of varieties of chilli, so you have loads of room for experimentation! Among my favourites is "Hungarian Black", which has purple flowers that lead to gorgeous, shiny, red fruits that slowly morph into inky black. The heat is reasonably mild (5-10k Scoville heat units) and the flavour is nicely rich. "Apache" is a great, dwarf variety that is ideal for a smaller space and produces an abundance of small, hot, red chillies that can hit 75k on the Scoville scale.

You can also just take the seeds from a supermarket chilli and plant those! I have done that with success, although I find the exciting range of non-supermarket varieties too tempting not to try a few new ones each year as well!

Two excellent chilli varieties: "Hungarian Black" and "Apache"

FRENCH AND RUNNER BEANS

Climbing (pole) beans are enormous plants that you would expect to find sprawling up huge eight or ten feet poles in a traditional kitchen garden. If you happen to have a balcony, you might try growing these up a wigwam of canes or a trellis. For the rest of us, thankfully both runner beans and French beans come in bush (dwarf) varieties that can be grown indoors in containers.

You can sow into the final growing site or start seeds off in small pots. Toilet roll inners also work, as per broad beans. A container 30-45 cm (12-18") wide is sufficient, and with some varieties you might manage to squeeze in a couple of plants per pot. Push each bean in a couple of inches deep.

Beans are thirsty, so keep them moist, and giving them a little feed once flowers start to appear will encourage lots of juicy pods to form.

Bush beans don't normally need support, although you can insert sticks or twigs to raise the beans away from the growing medium, if you wish. All green beans are best picked when young and tender. For runners, that typically means six to eight inches (20-30cm) in length, and for French beans, four or five inches (10-13cm).

For French beans, "Boston" is a bush variety that does well in containers, and for something a little different "Purple Teepee" has very attractive purple pods (although they turn green on cooking). For runners, "Hestia Dwarf" produces lots of long, tasty, stringless pods on a compact plant.

TOMATOES

Tomatoes are a fantastic choice for an apartment garden. They are straightforward to grow and even just one or two plants can give you a prolific harvest.

They come in two types, which reflect the growing form of the plants. Cordon (indeterminate) tomatoes grow to six feet tall or more and require a growing support. As such, unless you have a sunny balcony or a lot of floor space in a very light room for a large pot, these are probably not the most appropriate for your apartment garden. Bush (determinate) varieties, on the other hand, are much more compact and are ideal on a sunny windowsill or in a window box. They generally don't require support, unless the fruits become very heavy.

Tomato seeds need some warmth to germinate – 18°C (64°F) is ideal – but this generally isn't a problem indoors. You can use a propagator to help them along if you like, or cover them with a clear plastic bag and pop them on a warm windowsill. Sow from January to March or buy mature plants in summer. Once the seedlings appear, take off the bag or propagator lid and give them lots of light so they don't become leggy. Prick them out into individual pots after a few weeks.

The final container for bush tomatoes should ideally be 8-12" wide to give their roots plenty of room. If you're growing them in a trough or window box alongside other plants, allow 16" or more for each tomato to spread. Some bush tomatoes have a more upright form, whereas others are trailing varieties, so you may want to consider which would be best for the space you have in mind.

It's important to water tomatoes regularly, especially while fruiting, to stop the fruit from splitting and prevent a condition called blossom end rot that damages the fruit. Feed the plants with a tomato fertiliser or liquid seaweed feed every two weeks once the fruits start to form, to ensure a bumper crop. Harvest fruits individually once they are fully coloured.

There is a brilliant range of tomato varieties, and even when you are just growing determinate forms, there are many colours, shapes and flavours of tomato to experiment with. "Red Alert" is a heavy cropping cherry tomato with sweet fruits that are equally good in salads and in cooking. "Incas" is a plum tomato with a bush form, and the fruit has a substantial, meaty texture that makes it great for grilling and barbequing. "Tumbler" and "Tumbling Tom" are, as their names suggest, trailing varieties of bush tomato that look great spilling out of pots and they both produce prolific crops of small, sweet, cherry tomatoes. "Tumbling Tom" also comes in a yellow version. If you do have space to try a cordon variety, "Moneymaker" is ever popular for its reliable yield of mid-sized fruit.

Some tomato varieties: left to right, Tumbling Tom; Incas; Moneymaker

SWEET PEPPERS

As sweet peppers are very closely related to chillies, much of the approach to growing them is similar. One difference is that sweet peppers are more tender than most chillies and are even more fond of a warm environment. Whereas you might grow chillies outside on a balcony or in a window box through summer, sweet peppers are best grown inside on a warm windowsill.

Like chillies, sweet peppers need warmth to germinate and you can do the trick with the clear plastic bag covering to help them along until they sprout. To get decent sized fruits, sweet peppers call for a larger container than chillies: each plant ideally needs a foot (30cm) or more of growing space. As with chillies, feed once a week once the flowers appear and stake the plants when they look like they need it. They will also thank you for a spritz with a spray bottle for humidity purposes. If you pinch out the tip(s) of a plant when it reaches around 8" (20cm), that will encourage more side shoots and thus more fruit.

As with chillies, you can harvest sweet peppers when they are young, thus encouraging more fruit to form, or let them mature. They can come in red, yellow, orange and purple varieties and are green (or sometimes white) when immature.

"Tarquinio" yields well in containers and has quite square fruit that mature to a rich red colour. "Amy" gives a good harvest of smaller, pointed, red fruits. You could also try sowing seeds cut out of a supermarket pepper.

MUSHROOMS

Mushrooms may not be the first things that spring to mind when you think about growing your own veg indoors, but it's actually very doable to cultivate them at home. It's fascinating to watch them grow and you can take your cooking to new levels with the freshest gourmet mushrooms you are ever likely to have eaten. You could try your hand at growing shiitake, portobellos, and even impress your guests with homegrown lions' mane. However, the easiest mushrooms to grow indoors are oyster mushrooms, of which there are several tasty varieties. Yellow, pink, grey, pearl and king oysters are all good choices for indoor growing.

A range of mushroom growing kits are available that contain everything you need to get started. These can be a good choice for your first foray as a fungi farmer, but if you love mushrooms and intend to grow them on an ongoing basis, there are more cost-effective options that we will come back to in a little while.

Most cultivated mushrooms are looking for similar conditions. They are not too fussy about light, as long as they are not baking in the sun. In the wild, most of them would be growing in dappled shade in a woodland setting. They like a temperature between 10-20°C (50-70°F) with 15°C (around 60°F) being optimum. These conditions might perhaps be served by a north-facing windowsill. While a fungus is initially colonising its growing medium, it will be happy somewhere warm and dark, like an airing cupboard, before being moved somewhere lighter to fruit. Mushrooms like their growing medium to be kept moist but not waterlogged.

To grow mushrooms without a kit, you can buy packs of spawn from specialist suppliers online and from some gardening catalogues. The spawn is typically grain that has been inoculated with mushroom spores. The traditional growing medium is well-rotted horse manure, which provides the rich, moist conditions that mushrooms love. It's available in bags from garden centres, and the smell is less intense than with fresh manure, but unless you have a spot out of the way somewhere, it's understandable if you don't fancy the idea of manure in your home! Luckily, there are other options for your growing medium.

STRAW

Oyster mushrooms grow very well on straw, which you can buy cheaply from a pet shop. Get yourself a polythene bag – a sturdy bin liner will do fine – or an old bucket with large holes cut in the sides, along with a spray bottle and your oyster mushroom spawn. It's a good idea to sterilise the straw before you begin, by soaking in boiling water to kill off anything that might compete with your fungus. Allow it to cool completely before use.

Fill the bag or bucket with the straw, spraying generously with water as you put it in, so that all the straw is thoroughly moist. Empty a packet of oyster mushroom spawn onto the straw and mix it in well, then seal the bag or put a lid or film on the bucket and leave it somewhere warm for about six weeks for the fungus to colonise.

If using a bucket, you don't need to do anything else except check from time to time that the straw is still moist and give it a spritz if not. The mushrooms should find their own way out of the holes in the bucket. If using a bag, cut a series of 2-3" (5-8cm) slashes in the bag after the six-week point to allow the mushrooms to emerge.

Once mushrooms appear, you can harvest them incrementally, as soon as the edges start to turn upwards, simply twisting them away at the base, and the fungus should go on fruiting for several weeks.

Oyster mushrooms grown on straw in a bucket

COFFEE GROUNDS

Another great growing medium for oyster mushrooms is used coffee grounds. The best way to get hold of a lot of these quickly is simply to ask a local coffee shop, who will be throwing away loads of the stuff each day. An ideal container here is an old ice cream tub (with lid), milk carton or a sturdy polythene bag. If you get hold of enough coffee grounds, you can also opt for a covered bucket again. Poke a few holes into your chosen container for aeration.

If you obtained your coffee grounds freshly and in bulk from a coffee shop, you should not need to sterilise them before use, as the brewing process will already have done that for you. However, if you saved them over time or have had them sitting around a while, you can microwave them for a couple of minutes and the steam will reduce the numbers of bacteria and wild fungi that may have accumulated.

You are looking for a ratio of about 5:1 grounds to spawn by weight, so if you have 250g of spawn, you need about 1.25kg of grounds. Use a clean mixing bowl to thoroughly combine the spawn with the grounds before pouring into your chosen container.

Keep the mushroom container in a warm place like an airing cupboard for around three weeks, then check how well the fungus has established. The smaller volume of container means colonisation is faster than for a big bag of straw. The fungus will establish its white mycelium – its version of roots – before it can fruit. Once you see the grounds are almost covered in white, you can make the holes, a couple of inches in diameter, for the mushrooms to grow out of. If you are using an ice cream tub, you can just take off the lid.

Put the container in the fridge or a cool spot for a couple of days to stimulate fruiting, then put it somewhere light.

Once the holes are made or the lid is off, you'll need to mist the exposed areas regularly (perhaps twice a day) to prevent drying out. As with the straw method, you should start to see mushroom growth that goes on for a few weeks and you can harvest as you go.

PAPER

In the wild, oyster mushrooms, like many types of fungi, are found growing on trees or rotting wood. Given that paper is made from wood pulp, it makes a good home for indoor oyster mushrooms. There are two tried and tested methods here and they both make for fun projects for kids and adults alike to grow a small number of mushrooms in an interesting way. You can either opt for a (new) toilet roll or a book! If using a book, opt for one that's less than ten years old, as some older books were printed with toxic inks.

Pop your book or toilet roll in a strong plastic bag, cover with boiling water and let it cool, then drain the excess. You'll need about 25g of oyster mushroom spawn for a toilet roll and 30-50g for a book, depending on its size. Cover evenly with the spawn; in the case of the book, you can put some between the pages too. Seal the bag and put it somewhere warm for a couple of weeks.

Once your chosen host is well covered with white mycelium, keep it in the fridge for a couple of days, then put it somewhere reasonably light and take it out of the bag. From this point on, remember to mist regularly. If using a toilet roll, place it on its side to stop it rolling off anywhere. A book can either be placed on its side or stood upright with the pages slightly splayed. The end result can be spectacularly sculptural once the mushrooms appear!

CHAPTER 4

HERBS

MEDITERRANEAN HERBS

A lot of our favourite culinary herbs hail from the Mediterranean region, and share very similar growing conditions, so we can treat them all in pretty much the same way. That makes life easier in our indoor herb garden!

The main Mediterranean herbs are:

- Rosemary
- Thyme
- Sage
- Oregano
- Marjoram
- Winter savory

They are all very easy to grow. You can start with seed or else buy established plants very affordably. To grow from seed, sprinkle seed thinly in pots or a seed tray and lightly cover. Transplant when they reach an inch or so in height. You can give them individual pots (4-5"/10-13cm will do; just pot them on if they get too large) or plant a few together in a larger container for a herby one-stop shop.

The main thing to know about growing Med herbs is that they are especially keen on good drainage. They hate sitting in water, so ensure the pot drains well and water only when the surface feels dry. We'll also talk about mixing suitable growing media to give Med herbs an extra helping hand with drainage in Chapter 9. You can also layer some drainage material in the bottom of containers toward the same end. Bits of polystyrene from packaging work well, as do the more traditional "crocks" of broken ceramics, if you happen to have dropped a plate or terracotta pot recently!

The other thing Med herbs appreciate is good light. A sunny windowsill or window box is ideal.

You can harvest a little at a time when you need them. These herbs are all perennial, so should keep going for a couple of years at least before they start to get a little tired and need replacing. They all take well from cuttings, so you can always make more plants without needing to buy any ever again!

BASIL

Basil is a superb annual herb, with so many uses in the kitchen. You can be adorning pizzas and making your own pesto in no time! It can be grown from seed or you can buy a supermarket plant and take cuttings if you like.

Like the Med herbs, basil appreciates good drainage. However, unlike them, while it does like warmth, it doesn't thrive in full sun, so avoid south-facing windowsills.

Harvest leaves individually by pinching them off and allow the rest of the plant to continue growing. As an annual plant, it will need replacing every year, but is still very economical when grown from seed or cuttings.

As well as the typical sweet basil you find in the supermarket, there are all sorts of funky varieties you can try, including the spicier Thai basil, the smaller-leaved Greek and holy basil varieties, and attractive, shiny, purple-leaved cultivars, such as "Dark Opal". I love Greek basil sprinkled on fresh, homegrown tomatoes drizzled with extra virgin olive oil. Heaven!

Some basil varieties: left to right, sweet basil; Thai basil; Greek basil; Dark Opal

CHIVES

Chives are perennial and easy to look after. Like the Med herbs, they prefer a warm and bright spot and good drainage, although they are a little fussier about the soil not drying out, so be sure to water regularly through the warmer months in particular.

You can grow chives from seed by scattering the seed thinly across a seed tray or small pot and covering very lightly. Water gently, put them somewhere warm to germinate and cover with a clear plastic bag until they start to sprout. Pot them on when they reach a few inches in height. Alternatively, you can buy mature plants. While they don't take well from cuttings, chives do form clumps that can then be split, so you end up with multiple plants.

To harvest chives, snip with scissors close to the base. Harvesting encourages the plant to regrow, so the more you cut, the more you get. You can eat the purple flowers as well as the stems, and they make an attractive garnish. If you don't eat the flowers, cut them off once they start to fade.

Grown outdoors, chives would naturally die back in winter and regrow in spring. When we grow them indoors, it can interfere with that cycle and they may not die back fully but perhaps just stop growing in the cooler months, or they may choose to die back at another time. If they do die back, wilting and turning brown, just cut them right back to the base and they should regrow.

CORIANDER (CILANTRO)

Coriander is native to the Mediterranean and Middle East, and like the Med herbs we looked at a little earlier, it appreciates good drainage and sun. However, because it is an annual, we have to look at it slightly differently to those perennial Med herbs. If coriander is exposed to hot or dry weather, it tends to panic, thinking it may soon die, so it wants to produce seed in order to reproduce before its short life ends. It will therefore "bolt", sending up flower spikes that then produce its seeds, and no longer wants to grow leaves for us.

We therefore need to make sure that the growing medium stays moist (although still drains well) and move it out of full sun on hot summer days, if we want to keep it producing leaves for longer. If you use a lot of coriander in the kitchen, it can be a good idea to sow it successionally, perhaps once a month, so you always have some younger coriander on the go when your older plant tires or eventually bolts.

When plants do bolt, you can leave them to form the seed so you can collect it either to grind and use in cooking or to sow for your next crop, if you like. Just bear in mind that it goes tall and floppy and takes a while for the seed to form and dry a little so it can be harvested, so you may not want it on prime display during that time! If you do want to save the seed, wait for it to turn brown then cut off the whole stem and dunk it face down into a paper bag. Tie the bag on and hang up the stem until the seeds dry out fully and fall off into the bag.

Coriander grows very easily from seed, and it's one that I'd recommend sowing directly into whatever container you ultimately want to grow it in. This plant really hates having its roots disturbed, so can be fussy about transplanting, which can cause it to bolt quickly. So I suggest you just sow it, thinly and evenly, where you want it, lightly cover with soil and water it in. You can even try using whole seed from the supermarket spice aisle, although you might get better results from the seed produced by a horticultural seed supplier. As with all the herbs, you can of course also buy established plants, but then you'll have to keep buying more, unless you save and sow the seed from your first plant.

To harvest, pick or cut off stems then strip off the leaves. Regular harvesting encourages more leaf production.

DILL

Dill is another annual herb and it needs to be treated in much the same way as coriander. It too dislikes having its roots disturbed, so is best sown directly to its final container, and it will bolt more quickly in hot and/or dry conditions. It is also similar to coriander in that both the leaves and the seeds are edible and useful in the kitchen. The little yellow flowers are also edible and look quite pretty sprinkled as a garnish or used in salads.

Dill can become quite a large and ungainly plant, so it's a good idea to choose a dwarf ("nano") variety for growing in containers, which will be much more compact. Cut the leaves regularly to encourage more leaves and delay flowering. If you want to save the dill seed, the process is the same as for coriander. Let the seed turn brown, then cut whole stems and hang them upside down with a paper bag tied on until the seeds are all harvested.

MINT

Mint is a very vigorous perennial plant and is super easy to grow. While you can grow it from seed, I've found it doesn't germinate too reliably, so I'd suggest buying small plants. Because it loves to spread out, either give it a big pot (8"/20cm plus) to sprawl in or periodically take it out of the pot and split the clump into two or several plants, which can each have their own pot.

Like chives, mint doesn't appreciate being allowed to dry out and will quickly wilt if it does, but picks up again readily. Pick leaves regularly to keep lots of young, fresh growth coming and if the plant flowers, cut the whole thing back to a couple of inches afterwards to regrow.

There is an astonishing range of varieties of mint. I've grown at least a dozen different kinds, from the fruity pineapple mint, banana mint and apple mint to rich chocolate mint and black peppermint. A lot of our cultivated mints come under the species *Mentha spicata* (spearmint or garden mint) or *Mentha x piperata* (peppermint). The 'x' in the Latin name of the latter indicates that it is a cross (hybrid), in this case of *Mentha spicata* and another mint called water mint (*Mentha aquatica*).

Many of the curiously flavoured mints – lime, chocolate, etc. – are peppermints. Garden mint has the broadest range of uses in the kitchen, but the others have their uses and can be fun to experiment with. For example, chocolate mint is great to garnish desserts and lime mint is great in a gin and tonic! A lot of mints also make good 'teas' (tisanes) when steeped in hot water, but the king in this department is probably a spearmint called "Moroccan Mint".

PARSLEY

Parsley is technically a biennial, with a two-year life cycle, but is typically grown as an annual. There are both curly- and flat-leaved varieties, but the latter are a little easier to grow and have a stronger flavour for culinary use.

Parsley can be sown direct to the final container, like coriander and dill, but is less fussy about transplanting than its annual Mediterranean compadres, so you can also sow in a seed tray and move seedlings on when they are large enough, so you can have lots of little parsleys on the go and ensure that each plant has enough space to thrive, which is about 6" (15cm) per plant. If you use a lot of parsley, it can be wise to sow some successionally every month or two, so you always have the next crop lined up when you exhaust the current plants through repeat harvesting.

Parsley likes to be moist, so water it well, particularly in the summer. A light application of liquid seaweed fertiliser as the plant matures will help to ensure a healthy flush of green leaves. Sometimes parsley leaves turn yellow under stress. If this happens, cut out the yellow leaves, check the moisture and consider feeding the plant.

To harvest, cut stems at the base. There are quite a few parsley cultivars available, each with different characteristics of taste intensity and form. I personally love the big, strong-flavoured, flat leaves of "Italian Giant", but as the name suggests, it isn't the smallest cultivar so needs a bit of space to sprawl in a large pot or trough. For a standard-sized leaf and more compact, bushier form, "Plain Leaved 2" performs well. If you want to try a curly-leaved parsley, then "Extra Curled Dwarf" and "Moss Curled 2" perform especially well in pots.

TARRAGON

You might perhaps be slightly less familiar with tarragon than some of the other herbs we've looked at, but I think it's a really good one to have around for the kitchen. It has a mild, slightly lemony, slightly aniseedy flavour that pairs well with fish and poultry.

Tarragon comes in two types, Russian and French. Russian tarragon is hardier, but French tarragon is considered to have a superior flavour for culinary use. Especially given that we aren't worried about frost indoors, the French sort is definitely the one to go for in your apartment kitchen garden.

Tarragon is a perennial and is best propagated by cuttings or splitting. So you should be able just to buy one tarragon plant in order to create unlimited future plants. If you buy an established plant with multiple stems, you should be able to lift it out of the pot, disentangle the roots a little then lightly pull apart the stems with roots attached, immediately giving you several plants for the price of one!

Keep your tarragon regularly watered but not waterlogged and put it on a sunny windowsill. It flowers quite unpredictably, but if you do see buds appearing, pick them off to keep the plant's focus on producing leaves. To harvest, snip off shoots, then pick the leaves off the stems. As with most of these herbs, regular harvesting encourages the plant to put on new growth.

CHAPTER 5

FRUIT

As well as vegetables and culinary herbs, you can also grow a good range of fruit in and around your apartment. A lot of them are lower maintenance than you might think, and it's really rewarding to be snacking on your home-grown oranges or whipping up a delicious dessert with strawberries freshly picked from your window box.

There are also some more exotic fruits that can be a little trickier to grow, but great fun to experiment with. Let's take a look at some of the options for getting fruit to your table with zero food miles!

BLUEBERRIES

Blueberry bushes can do well indoors, provided you have a nice spot for them to soak up at least six hours of direct sunlight a day. They are unlikely to fruit without that light, but you could always invest in a grow light to provide it artificially. We will look at grow lights in more detail later in the book.

All blueberries are fine in containers – in fact, I even grow my outdoor plants in pots at my allotment – but you can also get dwarf varieties that are particularly suited to a windowsill.

A lot of blueberry cultivars are self-pollinating, but almost all will produce more fruit if allowed to cross-pollinate with other varieties, so if you have room for two or three different types, you can support a higher yield. Encourage pollination in the same way we discussed for aubergines and chillies, by manually transferring pollen from the flowers of one bush to those of another, using a small paintbrush or cotton bud.

Blueberries are thirsty and hate drying out, so water regularly, but avoid waterlogging. These plants are also fussy about being in acidic soil, so if you plan to pot them on at any point, buy ericaceous compost, which has been formulated for acid-loving plants. Feed with a liquid feed every two or three weeks while flowering and fruiting. Harvest fruits individually once they are a rich, dark blue.

The other important thing to know about blueberries is that they perform much better if they experience cooler temperatures (0-7°C/32-45°F) in winter. This cool time is often referred to in terms of "chill hours" and the number of chill hours required depends on the variety. So if you do have a cooler spot – if not a balcony then perhaps a north-facing windowsill – to for them to chill over winter, it will help them along. If you are worried about this, choose a variety that needs fewer chill hours, such as "Sunshine Blue" (150 chill hours) or "Jewel" (200 chill hours) rather than one that requires 500 or 600 chill hours.

CITRUS FRUIT

Citrus trees are a joy to have around. They look great, with their appealing forms and dark, glossy leaves, and very often the foliage smells as good as the fruit. I grow kaffir lime for its tasty, aromatic leaves, and know that if I prune my lemon tree, both the room and my hands will be smelling lovely and lemony for some time afterwards. Most citrus trees also release fragrance when in flower, acting as a natural air freshener.

Then there's the reward of the citrus fruit itself, these tangy gems that hail from the heat of Asia and Australasia and that our supermarkets import, grown right here in our own homes. When you get to pick your first citrus fruit, it's a pretty special moment!

When we think of citrus, oranges, lemons, and maybe limes come to mind, and you can grow all of these, but the citrus genus is broad and also includes kumquats, citrons, grapefruits and pomelos. Some of those more unusual species, like kumquats, are actually very well suited to apartment growing, so you can grow some very interesting crops. The handy thing is that all citrus plants need pretty much the same treatment.

These trees are fine at room temperature, but they want a light spot. Make sure they receive at least six hours of direct sunlight per day. If you have a balcony, it's fine to take them outside in summer, but be sure to bring them back in or fleece them with horticultural fleece before frosts arrive.

Citrus trees hate being waterlogged, and it's best to let the soil surface dry out before watering each time. They're also fond of humidity, so a light misting now and then or use of a humidifier can help to keep them happy. A trick that I employ for all of my humidity-loving houseplants is to sit the pot on a plastic saucer, a few inches wider than the pot, which has been almost filled with gravel. Watering the gravel allows moisture to evaporate gradually and raise the relative humidity around the plant.

Feeding with liquid seaweed once a fortnight from spring through to autumn helps to encourage plenty of flowers, which in turn should hopefully mean fruit! When flowers do appear, it's a good idea to help pollination along by transferring pollen between flowers of the same plant or plants of the same cultivar using a small paintbrush or cotton bud.

Citrus can take quite different growing forms. Lemons and oranges are often trained into 'standards' with a tall, bare stem and a big ball of foliage and fruit sitting on top. These look formal and very attractive in the right setting. Standards don't necessarily have to be full-sized, six feet trees, but can also be cute, dwarfing varieties.

Small lemon trees can thrive in a pot

RASPBERRIES

Raspberries grow on canes, and most varieties are too tall to feasibly grow indoors. However, there are some very tidy compact bush varieties (sometimes advertised as "patio" varieties) that are ideal for a container. You still want to give them a foot (30cm) of growing width at a minimum to spread out.

As with the other fruit, raspberries need at least six hours of sunlight a day and fruiting can be helped along indoors by hand pollination of the flowers. Keep the soil damp but not waterlogged and fertilise once a month. Harvest when the fruit are deep red (or gold, depending on the variety).

Raspberries can either fruit in summer or autumn, depending on the variety, and this also affects how they need to be pruned each year. With summer-fruiting ("floricane") varieties, this year's fruit is produced on last year's growth, whereas autumn-fruiting ("primocane") varieties grow stems each year that produce fruit in the same year. So once fruiting has finished, we just prune to the base the old stems that just finished fruiting in the case of summer-fruiting raspberries, leaving the newer shoots they have produced, whereas we cut back all the stems of autumn varieties in winter and new ones will grow next year.

Some great patio varieties to try include "Ruby Beauty" (summer fruiting), "Sweet Sunshine" (summer fruiting) and the golden-fruited "Patio Gold" (autumn fruiting).

RHUBARB

Rhubarb is a pretty unusual plant to have indoors, but is very easy to grow, provided you have room for a big container. It needs a container at least a foot (30cm) wide and deep. You can buy rhubarb in a pot or as a bare root "crown" that you plant a couple of inches deep.

Rhubarb is technically a vegetable, as we're interested in the stem of the plant (don't ever be tempted to eat the leaves, which are poisonous) but it is like fruit in wanting at least six hours of sunlight per day.

Give a newly planted rhubarb a year to establish itself before harvesting any. To harvest, wait for a good amount of red to blush the stems, then hold a chunky stem near the base and snap it away from the crown. It should come away cleanly, and you can then trim off the base and the leaf. Leave a few leaves intact on the plant so the rhubarb can still produce enough energy to keep itself going.

If your plant is getting too big for its container, lift it out once it has gone dormant in winter, trim the roots a little and carefully split the crown cleanly into two with a knife or cleaver, so you now have two plants.

STRAWBERRIES

Strawberries are naturally compact and shallow-rooted plants, so they are well suited to containers. They perform well in window boxes and can look great with their fruits dripping out of hanging baskets or suspended pots.

They can be grown from seed, but are inexpensive to buy as established plants, either in a pot or as a "bare root" to be planted up. Like most fruits, strawberries should be given least six hours of sunlight per day, but apart from that, they are relatively unfussy and easy to grow. They prefer infrequent, deep watering; let the soil dry out a little between waterings, then give them a good soak, ensuring they can drain. As with other fruit grown indoors, hand pollination of the flowers will help to ensure good fruiting.

Your strawberry plants will produce long tendrils called runners, which are the means by which the plant propagates itself. Baby plants form at intervals along the runners and take root. When grown in a container, plants will just dangle these runners out of the pot in search of soil in which to root. Generally, you'll want to cut them off when they appear so the plant conserves its energy, but you might want to propagate the odd one or two by pinning the baby plantlets onto the surface of soil in a new pot until they take root, then cut them free.

Fertilise once a month with a liquid feed and harvest fruits once they are deep red and glossy.

PINEAPPLE

If you fancy trying something a little more exotic, how about a pineapple? These funky fruits can thrive indoors, are interesting to look at and will surely impress your guests. They take a little patience and the fruit will be smaller than your typical supermarket offering, but they are not difficult to grow, the results taste great, and it's quite a thrill to harvest your own, home-grown pineapple.

You'll need a good sized pot for a mature plant to thrive – at least a foot (30cm) wide and deep. That's about five gallons in volume. Unsurprisingly, as tropical plants, pineapples need at least six hours of direct sunlight per day and like moisture and humidity. If you have a bright bathroom windowsill, that's perfect. Otherwise, pick another bright windowsill and mist occasionally. Water whenever the soil surface starts to feel a little dry and, as ever, make sure there is good drainage. The trick of having a tray or saucer of moist gravel underneath the pot works well here, to let water drain easily from the pot and help with maintaining some humidity.

You can buy a pineapple plant from a nursery, perhaps even with a fruit already forming, but where's the fun in that? Instead, it's an exciting project (for adults and kids alike) to cultivate a plant from a supermarket pineapple.

PROJECT: PINEAPPLE

Grow your own fruiting pineapple plant using a store-bought fruit.

1. Buy a ripe pineapple with lush green leaves.
2. Slice the top off the fruit, close to the crown.
3. Trim any excess fruit from around the base of the leafy crown, to prevent rotting.
4. Peel away leaves from the bottom couple of inches of the crown.
5. Allow to dry for a couple of days.
6. Fill a 6" (15cm) pot with potting compost, push the crown in about an inch deep and firm the soil around it.
7. Water gently, then loosely cover the plant with a clear plastic bag to keep moisture in.
8. Remove the bag after two months, by which time roots should have started to develop.
9. After around six months, pot the plant on to its final container that has a diameter of at least a foot (30cm).

A fruiting pineapple plant

You do need some patience with pineapples, and a home-propagated plant will take at least two years to flower and fruit, and will only do so then if it is happy, but in the meantime, you have an attractive houseplant to enjoy!

CHAPTER 6
OTHER EDIBLES

There are other edible plants that you have the potential to grow in your apartment kitchen garden that do not fit clearly into the categories we have covered so far. These are slightly more unusual choices that are fun to grow, useful in the kitchen, and interesting to show off to your guests!

BEEF AND ONION PLANT

The "beef and onion plant" (*Toona sinensis*), also known as "Chinese mahogany", among other things, is a species of tree native to east and southeast Asia. It has a savory, oniony flavour that is likened to beef and onion crisps, making it an ideal garnish for a barbecue as well as tasty in salads. It can also be added to stocks, soups and stews. In China, it is used to flavour rice.

While a mature specimen can exceed eighty feet in height, we can grow it as a baby leaf vegetable. There is also the option to grow it on as a perennial, harvesting young leaves every spring.

You may be able to source one from a nursery, or you can grow from seed, but the latter can be a little tricky. If growing from seed, soak the large seeds in warm water for an hour, then lay them out on a wet towel for a week to germinate, dampening the towel again if it dries out. Then pot them on with a potting mix and water well. Start with a 9cm (3.5") pot, then upgrade as the plant grows.

Toona likes good drainage and prefers a sunny position. Feed every two or three weeks when new leaves are forming to encourage strong growth. Leaves are best picked when young and tender.

GINGER

Ginger is easy to propagate and care for. It makes a great houseplant because it appreciates warmth and doesn't ask for a lot of space, plus its foliage is attractive.

Buy a fresh piece of ginger from the supermarket, looking for one with plenty of "eyes" – the little yellow protrusions from which roots will form. If it is a large piece, you can break it into 2" sections. You can start each piece in its own 6" pot or plant several in a larger pot. Use a potting mix and almost bury the ginger, so just an eye or two is sticking out above the surface. Water well, then cover with a clear plastic bag and put in a warm, bright spot for a few weeks until sprouts appear. You can then take the bag off and keep the soil surface moist. Ginger appreciates some humidity, so placing its pot on a tray of wet gravel will help it along.

The ginger we planted was the rhizome of the plant, and this is of course what we are most used to in the kitchen. However, you can get more use from this plant. You may be familiar with stem ginger, which typically comes in a syrup and is used in desserts and baking, and indeed you can harvest your ginger stems and use them in this way. But in the Asia-Pacific region, stem ginger is used fresh, finely sliced and added to salads or used as a condiment in fish or chicken dishes. It can also be stirred into drinks for a fresh zing. You can typically begin to harvest stem ginger from around six months after planting.

If you are planning to harvest the rhizomes, you'll need to wait around eight months. You'll see them spreading over the surface of the soil and slowly swelling. You can harvest a section at a time using a sharp knife or scissors, leaving the rest to grow on. Freshly dug, the rhizomes are pale yellow, sometimes with a blush of pink. The flavour is mild and the texture crisp. You can eat them like this or store them (in the fridge or in a cool, dark place) so they start to dry out and the flavour intensifies to the level you would expect from your original, supermarket ginger. You can of course opt to replant your harvested rhizome in new pots to get more plants.

Potted ginger

MUSHROOM PLANT

The mushroom plant or "mushroom herb" (*Rungia klosii*) is unrelated to mushrooms, but tastes distinctly like them. The leaves of this bushy perennial from Papua New Guinea are mineral rich and can be eaten raw in salads or cooked to intensify their flavour. They can be added to soups and stews to impart an umami richness; toss in at the end of cooking to preserve the bright green colour.

Mushroom plants are easy to look after indoors. They like warmth, prefer shade, and are unfussy about watering as long as they don't dry out completely. In summer, they may produce pretty little blue flowers. They are fine to be kept trimmed in small pots, but will spread quite vigorously if given growing room. If your plant seems to be struggling, it can benefit from a liquid feed. Harvest leaves at any time.

STEVIA

Stevia rebaudiana has made a name for itself in recent years for the sweetener that can be made from its leaves as a sugar alternative. It is a perennial hailing from Brazil and Uruguay, where it has been used for centuries in tea as medicine. It likes a moist, humid environment and full or part sun. It is a little tricky to grow from seed, so it perhaps best bought as an established plant; once you have one plant, it can be propagated easily from cuttings.

To harvest, pinch out tips of the plant to encourage new growth. Remove any flower buds so the flavour of the leaves is not hindered. Do not feed more often than every couple of months, as too much nitrogen leads to too many leaves and weak flavour.

To make your own stevia extract to add to your drinks, you'll need to dry out the stevia leaves by hanging a bunch for a few weeks with a paper bag tied around it. Then chop the leaves finely, place them in a sterilised jar and cover with vodka. Put the lid on the jar and wait a couple of days for the stevia to infuse, then strain the liquid into a saucepan. Heat gently for half an hour without boiling, so the alcohol is burned off and the extract thickens slightly. You can then pour your extract back into the emptied jar or into a small, sterilised bottle and store it in the fridge.

VANILLA

You'd be forgiven for thinking that long, slender vanilla pods are some kind of exotic bean, and indeed, they are sometimes referred to as "vanilla beans". If you didn't already know, you'd be very unlikely to guess that they actually come from an orchid! Originally hailing from Mexico, *Vanilla planifolia* is the only edible fruit-bearing orchid.

It takes care and patience to get this plant to flower and fruit indoors, but it is possible, and given that vanilla is the second most expensive spice in the world (after saffron), you might think it a worthwhile endeavor!

The vanilla plant grows as a climbing vine and its penchant for high humidity and partial shade makes it a top contender to grow in your bathroom. As it takes five or six years for it to consider fruiting, you'd likely prefer to buy an established plant. When potting on, use a specialist orchid compost or blend multipurpose compost in equal proportion to sphagnum moss. The soil should be kept moist but not waterlogged.

As this is a climber, it will need support if it is to get to a size that can support fruiting. It needs to reach at least ten feet in length, which can be achieved by mounting a sturdy trellis on the wall and weaving the vine left and right as it grows. Fertilise the plant every two weeks in spring and summer.

If you get your vanilla plant to flower, it will need to be

pollenated by hand. The process is much the same as for aubergines and other veg, using a small paintbrush or cotton bud to transfer pollen between flowers. If you look closely at a flower, the pollen should be visible as a fine powder on the female part of the flower (anther). However, the male part (stigma) has a shield around it that will need to be peeled back in order to deposit the pollen from another flower. Pollenate in the morning for best results, and if successful, you should see pods forming within a week.

To harvest, wait for the tips of the pods to turn yellow, then snip the pods away with scissors. They will then need to be cured before you can use them. First, place them into a pan of boiling water for two minutes, then plunge them into cold water to blanche. Wrap them in a towel and leave for a couple of days to start to turn brown, then store them in a dry, well-ventilated area for a couple of months until they are brown and wrinkly; at this point they should smell great and are ready for use!

SAFFRON

As we've talked about the second most expensive spice, it's only right that we should consider the single most expensive spice by weight – saffron. Saffron strands are the stigmas of the saffron crocus (*Crocus sativus*). The main reason this spice is so expensive is that the harvesting of these strands is very labour intensive at a commercial scale. However, you can very readily grow a few pots of saffron crocuses on your windowsill and harvest them easily. A little saffron goes a long way in culinary use, so you can grow enough to treat yourself to a nice paella or perhaps some saffron bread. An added bonus is that the delicate flowers look very pretty.

Saffron crocuses grow from corms, which are fleshy, underground stems that look similar to a bulb. You can buy them from garden centres or seed suppliers. They may not explicitly be advertised as saffron crocuses, as they are also grown ornamentally in gardens; just make sure you are buying a true crocus (*Crocus sativus*) and not autumn meadow crocus (*Colchicum autumnale*).

The corms can be grown in a pot of almost any size, but look most effective when grown as clusters in 6-8" pots, with corms spaced close together. Use a potting mix, ideally putting a layer of gravel in the base of the pot for extra drainage, before topping up with the potting mix. Corms should be planted 2" deep with the pointy bit facing upwards. You will see the most reliable results if you plant them in autumn (fall) to flower in the spring. Window boxes are ideal places to plant crocuses, as the plants will be exposed to the natural seasonality they would experience outside. Alternatively, keep them on a cool windowsill somewhere out of the way until they start to put on green growth. You can then move them to another windowsill if you wish.

Saffron crocuses

Once growth begins, water every other day. When you see

flowers about to emerge, keep an eye on them daily, because it's important to harvest the saffron as soon as the flowers open. As they open, you will see three long strands of saffron stigma per flower, which you can harvest with tweezers and store in an airtight container.

PART III
GROWING PLACES

By now, you not only understand how to get things growing, but also hopefully have some idea of the sorts of plants you might want to include in your apartment kitchen garden. The next step is to decide where and how you want to set up your plants in and around your home, and this is the topic of Chapter 7.

Then, in Chapter 8, we'll consider some possibilities for growing things in spaces away from your apartment, from rooftop gardens to garden sharing and community garden schemes.

CHAPTER 7
APARTMENT GROWING ZONES

We can take what we already know about the space, light, and other requirements particular plants need to thrive, and start to think about the kinds of containers we want to use and where is best to position them.

In this chapter, we will look at some specific growing zones around your home, from windowsills and window boxes, to a balcony (if you have one), to your bathroom.

I also hope to inspire you to get creative with the kinds of container you use and how to present them, thinking not just about freestanding pots but also options for wall-mounted and hanging displays.

Let's take a tour of your apartment growing zones!

WINDOWSILLS

Windowsills are our go-to places to grow plants indoors, and these are spaces we really want to make the most of. While you can grow on any windowsill that's deep enough to support a container, the heat and light requirements of some of the plants we've discussed means it pays to know which directions your windowsills are oriented. If you don't happen to own a compass, you can work it out by finding your home on a map. The orientation of your home is also shown on the plan attached to the property deed.

The sun rises in the east and sets in the west, so east-facing windows get sun in the morning, while west-facing windows get it later in the day. South-facing windows get the most sun overall, so tend to be the brightest and warmest spots, whereas north-facing windows are a bit duller and cooler. All are useful! Fruit, Mediterranean herbs, and warm-season veg will all thank you for a south-facing windowsill, whereas cool-season veg like spinach and rocket are better off on other windowsills.

Windowsill herbs can be a real statement in colourful pots

You might also give a thought to convenience and aesthetics when planning your apartment kitchen garden. Plants that you most want access to for regular harvest, like your favourite herbs, are going to need a home in or close to your kitchen. You might choose the prettiest plants for prime display on your living room windowsill and opt to keep your seedlings in the moist environment of the bathroom.

When grown on a windowsill, many plants will naturally start to lean towards the glass as they seek out the light. Just give their containers a regular turn when this happens in order to keep the plants upright and stable. If it becomes a real issue, you can buy support sticks and loosely tie in a central stem with twine.

Some of the best edibles to grow on windowsills include:

- Herbs
- Bush (determinate) tomatoes
- Microgreens
- Chillies
- Spring onions (scallions)

WINDOW BOXES

You may have been lucky enough to move into a home that has window boxes already installed, but if not, it should be easy to fit some yourself. A window box is simply a trough (which may be wooden, plastic or metal) that sits near the base of the exterior of a window, either resting on an outside ledge or mounted just beneath. These containers can be handy extensions to your indoor kitchen garden.

Window boxes would traditionally be mounted on metal brackets screwed to the exterior wall, but these can be a little tricky to install in an apartment setting and, if you rent, would likely require landlord permission. However, all is not lost, as window box brackets are available online that require no fittings whatsoever; they simply slot in snugly beneath your closed window. If your home happens to be clad with vinyl siding, there are also hooks available that allow containers to be easily suspended from the sidings.

Window boxes can be filled with bounty

Window boxes tend to be narrow and fairly shallow, so lend themselves to relatively small crops that don't need to establish extensive root systems. Some great choices here include:

- Cut-and-come-again lettuce
- Radishes
- Baby carrots
- Perennial herbs, such as rosemary
- Lavender, which smells great when you open the window and has culinary uses
- Spinach
- Saffron crocuses

BATHROOM

Your bathroom offers more humid conditions than much of the rest of your home, which is a boon to particular plants, although frosted glass or smaller windows can bring limitations in terms of light. So generally, we are looking for plants that like moisture and humidity and are okay without full sun. Some great options here are:

- Pineapple
- Fig
- Vanilla orchid
- Mint

BALCONY

If you live in an apartment with a balcony, you have a bonus space in which to grow edibles. A south-facing balcony is the jackpot, but any outdoor area is useful.

If your balcony does get plenty of sun, it can be used in summer for warm season crops like tomatoes. The extra height available versus windowsill or window box growing means you can try indeterminate tomato varieties, which grow taller and tend to produce larger fruit than bush varieties. Citrus trees can be taken out in summer to make the most of the warmth, light and insect-pollination opportunities.

Do think about how you can make use of the vertical space a balcony provides; for example, you might attach pots or troughs to the railings (there are even special troughs designed to sit on railings) or you might incorporate a trellis to grow climbing beans. Hanging baskets are a great option for strawberries, herbs and trailing tomatoes. You can also get multi-tiered grow stands that help to make the most of the available space and light.

A balcony can be a very useful growing space

In cool seasons, or year round on shadier balconies, you can grow plenty of spinach, rocket (arugula) and lettuce, as well as other cool-tolerant crops like beetroot and kale.

You may also want to take advantage of balcony floor space for edibles that require larger containers, such as rhubarb or blueberry bushes. You might also have a big pot of mint, which will thank you for the extra space to sprawl.

WALLS AND CEILINGS

If you own your own home or have your landlord's permission to attach fixtures to walls and ceilings, there is another range of creative possibilities for you to maximise your indoor growing space with attractive container displays.

Look out for wall-mounted containers or "green wall" growing pouches designed for indoor use. You may also find vertical grow stands that could work for you. Another option is simply to install some shelving and buy or upcycle some nice pots to put your edibles on display.

A pot hanging from the ceiling can look great with strawberries or herbs like prostrate (trailing) rosemary bursting forth. You may have heard of the art of macramé, which involves tying decorative knots in rope or textiles. This opens up some very appealing options for suspending pots. You can buy pre-made macramé hangers or get yourself a kit and have a go at making them yourself. There are also possibilities for getting creative with upcycling, such as by using old shoelaces and a yoghurt pot.

Prostrate rosemary in a hanging macramé pot

When choosing positions, pay attention to the light provided by your windows throughout the day. It is also generally best to avoid locating your containers above radiators or a fire, as they can dry out quickly.

Plants that are good contenders for small wall-mounted or hanging pots include:

- Herbs, especially types that will trail attractively, like prostrate rosemary and creeping thyme
- Lettuce
- Strawberries
- Microgreens

CHAPTER 8

ABOVE AND BEYOND

We've now considered a wide range of edible plants and looked at different ways you can grow them to make the most of the spaces available in and around your apartment. Before I leave you to your gardening adventures, I want to mention some possibilities for accessing growing spaces outdoors, even if you have no garden or balcony of your own. Outdoor gardening offers the prospect of fresh air and exercise, as well as more growing space, and there are ways to make your garden a social experience too. Let's look at some options.

ROOFTOP GARDENING

As people have sought to create more green spaces and grow food in urban areas, rooftop gardening has been growing in popularity. The flat rooves of many apartment and office blocks lend themselves to planting, and their elevated position means they typically receive both good sunlight and rainfall, as well as experiencing fewer pest and weed problems than gardens on the ground.

A rooftop garden can be as simple as a few plants in pots or as elaborate as a set of irrigated raised beds with seating areas. You could set something up yourself or form a project with neighbours or work colleagues. If you live in an apartment building or condo, you'll just need to check beforehand with the building owner or condo association to see if they'll permit plants in the shared space on the roof. There may also be weight and height restrictions to consider.

When it comes to planting, take note of sunny and shady spots and choose your plants accordingly. For example, tomatoes, Mediterranean herbs and leafy greens will all appreciate the warmth, whereas spinach and rocket (arugula) prefer somewhere a little cooler.

Aside from regular watering, the other key thing to be

mindful of on a rooftop garden is the wind. Depending on the aspect and the surrounding buildings, rooftops can sometimes be breezy places, and a lot of plants dislike that kind of exposure. Feel which directions winds tend to blow from and introduce a windbreak, which might be a simple, low fence or trellis, or perhaps a row of small conifers in terracotta pots.

You could look online at the rooftop gardens others have made to draw inspiration, then get creative with the possibilities! If your building is unsuitable for rooftop gardening or you cannot get permission, shared apartment yards or gardens can sometimes present additional planting spaces too, plus there are other options further afield.

COMMUNITY AND ALLOTMENT GARDENS

Cities, towns and villages across many parts of the globe feature community gardens, often with the goal of growing food. In Britain and parts of Europe, we tend to distinguish community gardens as collective endeavours from allotments, which are parcels of land split into smaller plots for individuals or families to lease. In the US, the distinction is less clear, and most community gardens are in fact divided into individual plots. They can be owned by public bodies, non-profits or private landowners and can vary widely in both cost and terms of lease.

Check online or ask around to see if there is a community garden scheme or allotment site near you. You may be surprised at what is out there. If there is nothing going on nearby, you could even try to set up your own community garden.

An allotment or community garden plot offers expanded possibilities

For some inspiration, take the example of Ron Finley, whose impressive efforts to encourage local communities to grow their own food have garnered him an international reputation. In 2010, Ron dug up a section of land outside his home in Los Angeles, between his house and the curb, and planted fruit and vegetables there. When officials told him it was illegal to use that space for growing food, he got the law changed. He scouted unused spaces around LA where things could be grown, and established dozens of community gardens. The self-styled "gangsta gardener" set up a non-profit organisation to promote urban gardening and has travelled widely, educating individuals and communities about how to set up their own projects. His TED talk has been watched by millions, and I can recommend that you join them!

As well as allowing you to grow and harvest more food, being part of a community garden is a social opportunity to spend time with likeminded people, and there is increasing awareness that gardening is good for mental health as well as physical exercise. I go to my allotment to unwind, listen to the birds, look after my plants, breathe some fresh air and get stuck in to some weeding or start my creative juices flowing on a new project. I always grow extra plants and produce to give to others on the site and usually receive some in return, plus we share tips, have discussions and hold meetings down the local pub.

Each year, it's exciting to plan my planting and pick out new varieties to try, and with the help of a greenhouse, I'm able to produce a good amount of my fruit, veg and herbs, year round. Signing up for an allotment was one of the best decisions I ever made. You may find that sites in your areas have a waiting list for plots, but it will be worth the wait. In the meantime, there is another option...

GARDEN SHARING

Another great way to access more land for gardening is to sign up with one of the many garden sharing networks. The basic premise is simply to find someone who has a garden or some other land that they can't or don't want to tend, and connect them with someone else who is looking for space to grow things. Lend and Tend operates nationally in the UK, and Shared Earth does the same thing across the USA, but there is also a wealth of local organisations in these countries and elsewhere.

Garden sharing is usually an individual arrangement, but larger pieces of land can also sometimes be managed by groups or communities, making it another route to community gardening. Depending on the network you use to locate a host garden, the agreement with the owner might be very informal or there might be a contract in place. Either way, it's a good idea to make sure that you are both clear and in agreement about expectations.

In particular, you need to determine who provides equipment and supplies and what happens to the produce. There may also be some ground rules about acceptable behaviour and what you are allowed to do with the site. You do not normally have to pay to use the land, but may agree to share a proportion of the produce with the owner.

PART IV
TAKING THINGS FURTHER

My aim so far in this book has been to prime you with the basic knowledge to start growing a wide range of edibles with minimal equipment and a minimal budget. I wanted to keep things simple and avoid a focus on buying lots of gear. After all, a little canny upcycling here and there while growing most of your plants from seed or inexpensive starter plants means you can grow plenty of food without breaking the bank.

However, once you are confident with the basics, you might decide to think about ways of boosting your yields, extending your harvests, and optimising the health of your plants through some slightly more advanced techniques that make use of additional equipment or inputs. Not all of these are necessarily very expensive, and the pricier bits of kit can make good investments over time, especially if the layout of your home doesn't naturally present you with ideal growing conditions.

In Chapter 8, we're going to look at mixing your own growing media to create the ideal environment for your plants to root in, as well as making your own compost. Then, in Chapter 9, we will think about the role that artificial lighting and heating can play in getting the most out of your crops, and also consider the possibilities for growing hydroponically.

CHAPTER 9

SOIL SCIENCE

Understanding and creating good soil is a science in its own right, but when it comes to apartment kitchen gardening, we don't need to make things too complicated.

Using what we know about the requirements of different plants at different stages of their lives, we can easily create growing media that are good enough approximations of the soil conditions of their natural environments, helping them to thrive.

We can also enrich our plants with our own, homemade compost, even when gardening indoors. Let's try a little apartment alchemy...

MIXING MEDIA

Back in Chapter 1, I talked a little about the difference between compost and soil, as well as mentioning the importance of using the right growing medium. You may recall that I explained that while you can use multipurpose compost for some things, it's often not ideal on its own. For simplicity, I suggested you could buy specific pre-mixed media from the garden centre, such as a seed mix for sowing finer seeds and a potting mix for potting on. These mixes are an improvement over multipurpose compost, but you can exert greater control over your growing media and possibly also save money by making your own mixes. You can create custom mixes to suit particular plants at particular stages in their lifecycle.

There are many possibilities for media ingredients that can be combined to closely mimic particular soil environments, but just four common components can help us create media for most purposes:

- Multipurpose compost – great as a base for many mixes. Choose peat-free for a greener choice when you can. You can also use coir (coconut fibre) in

mixtures instead, or your own homemade compost (see the next section).
- Grit – you can buy horticultural grit, but any fine grit such as 10mm gravel will do.
- Vermiculite – a natural mineral heated to a high temperature to form lightweight flakes. It improves aeration, drainage and nutrient delivery to plant roots. You can also use perlite for aeration and drainage, but it gives off a fine white dust when moved around, so I don't recommend it for indoor use.
- Sand – buy horticultural sharp or silver sand or any sharp sand, but not building sand, which contains unwanted elements.

Combinations of these ingredients can result in great growing media for a variety of situations. Get yourself a large pot, bowl or tray in which to mix the media well before use. I also suggest either buying a plastic scoop or making an upcycled one out of an old drinks bottle, to make it easier to move ingredients and measure proportions.

You can of course scale the amounts of each ingredient up or down in proportion, depending on how much you need. These ratios are not set in stone and you can adjust them as you think necessary.

SEED MIX

A mix for starting seeds. Most seeds prefer a loose, open compost that is not too rich.

- 1 part multipurpose compost
- 1 part vermiculite

CUTTING MIX

A mix for encouraging cuttings to root. Richer than a seed mix, to promote new growth, but still with all-important drainage and aeration to reduce the risk of cuttings rotting before they strike. Dipping the base of the cutting into rooting hormone before planting will improve its odds of survival.

- 2 parts multipurpose compost
- 1 part vermiculite

POTTING MIX

For when you come to pot on seedlings, rooted cuttings or established plants. This contains more nutrients than our seed mix, and provides a good balance of drainage, aeration and moisture retention.

- 2 parts multipurpose compost
- 1 part vermiculite
- 1 part grit or sand

MEDITERRANEAN MIX

For plants that hail from a Mediterranean climate, including all of our Med herbs, figs and lavender. These plants can be especially fussy about having very free drainage, so it helps if we increase the ratio of sand or grit compared to a standard potting mix. You can also optionally add a further layer of grit to the base of the container before potting up.

- 2 parts multipurpose compost
- 1 part vermiculite
- 2 parts grit or sand (or 1 part of each)

HOMEMADE COMPOST

The thought of homemade compost might bring to mind great steaming mounds of decomposing matter in a gardener's outdoor composting bays, but it's perfectly possible to make good compost on a small scale inside your home. Home composting is a great way to recycle food waste into a rich, organic medium that will help your plants to thrive. And don't worry – done correctly, it shouldn't be steamy or smelly.

The fastest method for making compost indoors is to enlist the help of worms to make vermicompost. You can do it without the worms, but it will happen much more slowly.

You may have heard of "bokashi composting", which has become quite a trend and is sometimes promoted for people in apartments. The thing to know here is that bokashi, a rapid fermentation process hailing from Japan, does not produce compost. Instead, the fermentation partially breaks down food scraps and produces a liquid that can be used as a fertiliser. The fermented scraps then have to be thrown away or composted elsewhere. They are not, however, well received by worms, who dislike anything acidic, so aren't suitable for worm composting. Thus, I wouldn't recommend bokashi in an apartment when vermicomposting is cheaper and gives us useful compost as well as liquid fertiliser.

WORM COMPOSTING

You can buy a worm composting bin or make one yourself; I'll explain how to do the latter in a little while. To get your vermicomposting operation started, you'll need worms, water, shredded paper and about a pound (half a kilo) of compost. The best worms for rapid composting are "red wrigglers", which are readily available online. They will breed and multiply, so you should only need to buy one batch. A pound of (half a kilo) of worms will be enough. Do not buy "Asian jumping worms" (a.k.a. "Alabama/Georgia jumpers"), as they are an invasive species. For the paper, you can use newspaper or any paper that isn't glossy or coloured.

Soak enough shredded paper to cover the bottom three inches of your bin, then combine it with the soil in the bin and add the worms. Give them a day to settle before feeding them.

Using this method, you can compost:

- Raw vegetable and fruit peelings and scraps
- Coffee grounds
- Tea bags (unless plastic)
- Egg shells
- Prunings from your plants

However, you cannot include:

- Meat, bones, or any other animal part
- Dairy products
- Cooked food

Worms are also not very fond of acidic food, like citrus and members of the allium family (especially onions and garlic), so these are best kept to small amounts and chopped up into small pieces or omitted altogether. Too much acid can harm and even kill the worms. You will get to know your worms' tastes; if you see after a week that the worms have clearly rejected something, just take it out.

It is best to avoid disturbing your worms too much, so save up your food scraps for a week in a separate bin, then feed them to your worms in one go on the same day each week. Each time you add a batch of scraps to the compost, cover them completely with more shredded paper, as well as with a layer of compost if you have some to spare, then put the lid back on. Keeping the scraps covered will discourage fruit flies from becoming a nuisance.

When your bin is getting full and the compost is looking ready, start adding food just to one side for a couple of weeks to draw the worms across before extracting the compost from the other side. Then start building scraps in the base of the side you emptied to draw the worms across that way before extracting the compost on the remaining side. If you bought a bin with layered trays, the process is essentially the same: start a new layer to draw the worms before emptying the full one.

You can use your compost right away or store it in a bag or another bin. Every few months, you will need to drain out the liquid that collects in the liquid compartment or in the lower bin (if your wormery is homemade). This "worm tea" makes a great fertiliser for your plants.

You can keep your wormery anywhere you like indoors, as long as the space is between 16-28°C (60-80°F), but worms have a preference for somewhere dark and quiet. The entire process takes three to six months.

If your household produces a large volume of kitchen

waste, you may do better buying a wormery with several tiers, which also allows you to extract a smaller amount of compost more frequently. However, if you won't have mountains of scraps to compost each week, it's a straightforward and inexpensive project to make your own simple worm bin.

PROJECT: WORMERY

MAKE A CUSTOM BIN FOR WORM COMPOSTING

A basic, homemade wormery

You will need:

- Two plastic containers, one taller and narrower than the other, so it rests inside but sticks out. The

tall one needs a lid; the other does not. Ideal sizes are 15"d x 25"w x 5"h and 15"d x 20"w x 15"h
- A drill and two drill bits—1" and 1/8" diameter
- Vinyl screening material (used for window screens)
- Waterproof glue

1. Drill a 1" hole in one side of the taller bin, about 2" from the top. Repeat on the opposite side.
2. Drill four 1/8" holes in the base of the same bin, near the corners.
3. Cut squares of vinyl to cover the holes with some overlap and glue in place.
4. Place the tall bin inside the shorter bin and let the glue dry before using.

CHAPTER 10
ADVANCED EQUIPMENT

If you are looking for ways to boost your edible yields, extend your growing seasons and maximise the growing space in your home, you may be thinking about some slightly more advanced equipment to help you along. Or maybe you just love a good gadget. Either way, this chapter will prime you with some useful pointers about what to look for.

We will look in turn at artificial lighting, heating, and the curious world of hydroponics.

GROW LIGHTS

If your edibles are struggling to get enough sunlight to thrive, either during the winter, in shadier spots or simply because the climate where you live is ill-suited to warm season crops, you have the option of introducing artificial grow lights. You can also use grow lights to extend the natural growing season, giving a head start to slow-maturing, light-loving plants like tomatoes.

It's important to understand that when it comes to aiding plant growth, not all lights are made equal. The colour temperature and intensity of light matter, as does the amount of heat produced, and the purchase cost and energy efficiency (and thus cost to run in terms of electricity usage) can be factored in too. You need to get the right kind of light, and there are two main types that are suitable for indoor growing.

T5/T8 high output (HO) fluorescent tubes have long been used for grow lighting. The "T" simply refers to their tubular shape and the 5 and 8 refer to their diameter in eighths of an inch. They are relatively inexpensive, their light is intense enough to support growth, they give off little heat (so can safely be positioned close to plants) and they last a long time (about 20,000 hours). They're also fairly energy efficient.

LED grow lights are now becoming more popular as a challenger to T5/T8 HO tubes. They bring the same collection of technical benefits but are more energy efficient and even longer lasting than fluorescent lights. Initially, they were more expensive, but prices have come down a lot as this technology has spread in uptake.

In terms of colour temperature (the measure of colour in a light source), plants are mostly interested in red and blue light, which are found at the two extremes of the visible spectrum. Reddish hues are found from around 2700-4000 Kelvin (K), whereas bluish hues come in from around 5000-7500 K. Red light aids flowering and fruiting, whereas blue light is good for vegetative growth.

Both fluorescent and LED lights are available in different colour temperatures. For leafy vegetables and herbs, like lettuce or parsley, a 7500 K light will support that green growth. For crops that you want to flower (and thus fruit), like courgettes (zucchini) or tomatoes, you might use a 7500 K light together with a 4000 K one to support strong growth of the plants and their fruit. You can also buy systems that are already set up with a combination of colour temperatures.

LED lights are often advertised as "full spectrum", which implies they emulate the full spectrum of natural sunlight, offering a simple, catch-all solution. They usually have a colour temperature of 6500K to mimic daylight. However, "full spectrum" is not a clearly definable term and these lights might not bring any added benefits to plants versus other lights in a similar colour temperature range. Points of note here are that the sun's radiation is actually widely dynamic, changing a lot through the course of a day and across seasons, and also a lot of the spectrum is useless to plants. We just need to focus on getting the plants what they need. Full spectrum LEDs are fine for bluish light for growth, but don't pay over the odds thinking that the full spectrum claim is going to do anything special for your plants.

You may see other types of light advertised as grow lights, such as high pressure sodium systems and metal halide lights. These are classified as high intensity discharge (HID) lights and are not a good choice for home use, because the immense heat they produce means both that they require more space to avoid damaging plants and that they call for extraction equipment to remove the hot air. Stick with T5/T8 HOs or LEDs.

Larger lighting units can be a considerable investment, but a couple of fluorescent tubes or a simple LED light bar will often be sufficient to give your plants the boost they need.

HEATING

Given that your home likely remains warm for much of the time, you probably don't need to introduce further heat for the great majority of your edible plants to thrive, and heat tends to be much less of a limiting factor for indoor gardening than light. However, there are still some situations where you might want to employ some extra heating.

One of the key times when heat is especially important is when trying to germinate the seeds of warm-season plants like chillies, sweet peppers, aubergines and tomatoes. While you may be able to germinate them on a windowsill, especially as the seasons warm, you will get the best out of your growing season if you can start them off early, towards the end of winter. To help do that successfully, heat mats and heated propagators are our friends.

If you are looking to expand growing seasons, or boost the yield of heat-loving plants, or perhaps if you have no central heating, you may also consider using a heat mat for these reasons, perhaps in combination with grow lights.

Both heat mats and heated propagators can also be used to give a helping hand to cuttings.

HEAT MATS

A heat mat is a very simple piece of apparatus that consists of a heating element inside a flexible (typically plastic) mat. You plug it in, lay it on a windowsill or other bright spot and line up your trays, pots or unheated propagators on it to receive a gentle warming from beneath.

They come in different sizes and qualities, but a basic, small one shouldn't be very expensive. They can come with or without a thermostat to set the heating to a specific temperature. It's not the end of the world if you get a mat without a thermostat, as it will still provide a boost and should be limited so it cannot get too hot. If you do get one with a thermostat, setting a temperature of 25°C (around 75°F) is ideal for germinating most warm-season veg.

There are two important things to be aware of when using a heat mat for germination. One is that the extra heat will dry out your growing medium more quickly, so you need to keep an extra eye on the watering, especially if using uncovered containers. The other is that while the extra heat is great for stimulating germination of our warm-season crops, it is not so great for seedlings, as they tend to become leggy and floppy instead of strong and stout. So, as soon as you see the seedlings sprouting, either gradually reduce the thermostat, if you have one, by five or six degrees over the following days, or else take the container off the heat and let it sit on a bright windowsill.

HEATED PROPAGATORS

I'm writing this in February and right now I already have tomatoes and chills growing a few inches tall thanks to my heated propagator. A propagator is little more than a seed tray with a transparent lid. It is designed to act as a tiny greenhouse, retaining heat and moisture. Add an extra source of heat, and you have a little germination powerhouse. You can place a regular propagator on a heat mat, or you can by a specially designed heated propagator unit, which is perhaps a little more efficient with its heating and with your precious windowsill space.

The units come in different sizes and may comprise a single, larger propagator on a heated base, or several smaller ones. As with heat mats, heated propagators can come with or without thermostats, and once again, the high heat is only needed for germination, after which you can turn it down or off, or move your propagators off the heated base.

HYDROPONIC KITS

As we discussed in Chapter 1, hydroponics opens up the possibility of growing plants directly in water. We looked at the raft method as well as easy ways to grow herbs and resprout vegetables hydroponically, and I mentioned that you can also invest in kits, which is the part we're going to come back to now.

Hydroponic kits or systems are designed to make hydroponic growing convenient by combining a suitable container with a water reservoir and sometimes other features such as LED lighting and water circulation. The very simplest kits are designed for growing microgreens and consist of just a tray with some capillary matting as a growing medium. However, most are a little more sophisticated.

In allowing nutrients to be dissolved and delivered directly to roots, hydroponics offers the potential to grow lush plants very quickly. If artificial lights are involved, there is the further promise of extending that high productivity year round. That's certainly a tempting prospect. However, with a growing range of kits on the market, some reaching quite dizzying prices, it's worth knowing what the differences are and what to look for in choosing the right kit for you.

A small hydroponic kit with LED light

Some of the key feature differences you might come across include:

- Type – While systems generally involve a porous container of growing medium suspended in or above a water reservoir, they employ methods of varying complexity. You may see terms like "flood and drain", "aeroponic" and "Kratky method". These all bring subtle benefits and drawbacks, but it can be a little overwhelming to try to compare them all as a beginner. The other factors in this list should help you choose a kit that suits you, regardless of the precise method used. If in doubt, start with an aeroponic kit; these suspend your plants in air and spray the plants or roots with the nutrient solution, and they tend to be compact and easy to use.
- Size – Kits can vary from small, countertop units to multi-level racks to support dozens of plants. The size of plant supported also varies. It's also a

good idea to measure the space where you intend to locate your system and check how well different kits would fit.

- Water pump – Many kits come with a water pump, which is important when crops are going to spend a long time in water, both to circulate nutrients and prevent stagnation. However, some pumps can be quite noisy. Some kits therefore pride themselves on having a quiet pump.
- Lights – Some kits include LED lights to give your plants a boost. These are generally daylight or "full spectrum" lights, so you may still choose to use additional lights (refer back to the grow lights section). The power rating of LED lights can vary widely. On some models, the light unit is adjustable so it can be adapted to taller plants.
- Automation – Sometimes lights and/or the water pump are automated to come on only when needed.
- Monitor and indicators – Many kits come with indicator lights or digital screens that monitor the water level and/or nutrient levels, to let you know when to add water or plant food. Some kits even come with an app to help you monitor your inputs.
- Expansion possibility – Some kits have a modular or stackable design so you can easily expand the capacity of your unit, if and when you want to.
- Starter pack – Some kits come with starter seeds and/or plant food. There will typically be a substrate involved as the growing medium, such as coir, and you will usually be given a starting amount of this, often in the form of plugs. Kits that include plugs that already contain seeds offer a very convenient option for a beginner.
- Style and maintenance – Given that your system is

on show in your home, you might spare a thought for how the aesthetic of a unit suits your décor and taste. Some kits are also easier to clean and maintain than others; check out reviews for indications of practicalities like this.

So, as you can see, there are a few things to think about, but in reality, the range of features is broadly determined by budget, and if you want an all singing, all dancing model, it can wind up being pretty costly. You may think it sensible to start with a small kit to see whether or not you take to hydroponics before splashing out on more expensive gear. If you buy an expandable system, you can always add more capacity when you're ready.

CONCLUSION

I hope you are now determined that, even if you live in an apartment, you can still grow an impressive array of edibles in your home and beyond. From oregano to oranges to oyster mushrooms, you can have an entire kitchen garden at your fingertips. I hope you are keen to get stuck in with growing things, and know that it will be a pure joy when you begin harvesting fresh and tasty produce.

I hope you might also be feeling inspired to get creative with a project or two – perhaps an upcycled animal planter or a hanging macramé herb pot? And once you've mastered the basics and filled all your windowsills with abundance, maybe you'll even branch out beyond the apartment and think about a rooftop garden or some community gardening. Your gardening future is full of possibilities, and I wish you the best of luck.

If you have enjoyed reading this book and would like to recommend it to others, I would be grateful if you could leave a review on Amazon.

Happy kitchen gardening!
James Jacques